LIVING QUESTIONS.

THE

LIVING QUESTIONS

OF THE AGE.

BY AN AMERICAN CITIZEN.

AUTHOR OF "THE PHILOSOPHY OF THE PLAN OF SALVATION," "GOD REVEALED IN CREATION AND IN CHRIST," ETC.

CHICAGO:
CLARKE & CO.
PHILADELPHIA: CLAXTON, REMSEN & HAFFELFINGER
NEW YORK: SHELDON & CO.
BOSTON: LEE & SHEPARD.

1869.

A. B. Case, Printer, Chicago.

TO THE

YOUNG MEN

OF THE

CHRISTIAN ASSOCIATIONS

OF EVERY LAND,

These Pages

ARE RESPECTFULLY DEDICATED.

PREFACE.

In the following pages the author has endeavored to meet, in a popular form, some of the prevailing moral fallacies of the age.

It is admitted by every one who has observed the state of public opinion in relation to moral and religious questions, that no inconsiderable portion of the business men of our cities and villages—especially the young men—are influenced by opinions which are inconsistent both with sound reason and with revelation. This volume is an endeavor to bring back some who have wandered, to a rational apprehension of religious doctrine and duty.

It asks the forbearance of the dogmatic theologian. The effort of the author is to give the rationale of the Christian doctrines which he discusses. Those for whom these pages are mostly designed have chosen reason, rather than revelation, as arbiter in matters of faith. We have, therefore, permitted reason to speak freely in behalf of revealed truth, and to speak sometimes in forms of language that we would not use with those who are believers in divine revelation.

We have, in the discussion, waived all questions not involved in the main issues, and have granted to the opposers of evangelical religion all that a fair mind can ask; and as the skeptics of our day claim a philosophical basis for many of their opinions, we have endeavored to meet them on their own ground.

"Prove all things; hold fast that which is good," is a Scripture precept.

The discussion covers the living issues of our times between the friends and opponents of evangelical Christianity. The draft of some of the chapters was originally in the form of letters to a friend, well known in literary circles at the east. This will account for occasional peculiarities of phraseology. The quotations from "Discourses of Religion," will be found mostly in the first two chapters of that work.

The style is as popular as the character of the subjects would permit. If it shall answer the ends of a hand-book on the subject of heterodoxy in religion and reform, the author's aim will be accomplished.

CONTENTS.

CHAPTER I.

Incongruity of the Skeptical and Theological Philosophy of Liberal Christians 11

CHAPTER II.

Variations and Contradictions in the Theological Opinions of Skeptical Unitarians and Transcendentalists.................................. 21

CHAPTER III.

Literary, Mystical, and Evangelical Aspect of Liberal Christianity.............................. 29

CHAPTER IV.

Better Phases of Liberal Christianity 45

CHAPTER V.

Development of Divine Revelation in the three Dispensations of Power, Law and Love........ 65

CHAPTER VI.

Personality of God........................... 81

CHAPTER VII.

The Tri-unity of the Divine Mind.............. 102

CHAPTER VIII.

Human Depravity............................... 122

CHAPTER IX.

Reconciliation or At-one-ment with God......... 142

CHAPTER X.

Future Retribution............................ 161

CHAPTER XI.

Refutation of common Fallacies on the subject of Future Retribution......................... 182

CHAPTER XII.

Written Revelation a Necessity in order to the Moral Development and Moral Progress of Mankind.................................. 191

CHAPTER XIII.

Divine Revelation the Motive Power in Human Progress.................................. 212

CHAPTER XIV.

Reformers and their Relation to Christianity..... 248

CHAPTER XV.

Woman's Rights, Woman's Suffrage............. 255

CHAPTER XVI.

Capital Punishment........................... 282

CHAPTER I.

INCONGRUITY OF THE SKEPTICAL AND THEOLOGICAL PHILOSOPHY OF LIBERAL CHRISTIANS.

From the time of Dr. Priestley until now, those who have departed from the evangelical faith have devised various schemes of theology and philosophy, which they have presented for the acceptance of the world. Some of these have contained good suggestions, and some of them criticisms of orthodox views that were needed; others have been wanting both in reason and congruity.

The last of these schemes is that of the late Theodore Parker, a writer of unusual ability, and of benevolent impulses. His opinions belong to the skeptical side of Unitarian, or Liberal Christianity. He was recognized, during his life-time, as an exponent of the opinions of his class; and although his influence upon the denomination is, perhaps, waning, still his works are the latest and most popular of the attempts to set forth a new theology and philosophy in regard to the knowledge of God and human duty. We have adopted his book as the best and latest exhibit of the theology of skeptical Unitarians; and the recent valuable work of Dr. Freeman Clarke as the last and best view of the evangelical side of Liberal Christianity.

In making an analysis and criticism of Mr. Parker's Unitarian scheme, we will note some passages in his "Discourses of Religion." They will sufficiently indicate the character of transcendental theologizing, and warrant any language which may seem to be severe in the ensuing paragraphs.

This liberal writer says, "The religious sentiment does not disclose the character, and much less the nature and object, on which it depends."

Again, "The sentiment of God, though vague and mysterious, is always the same in itself."

Again, we are told that "the idea of God comes of the joint and spontaneous action of reason and the religious sentiment."

Again, "The idea of God as a fact given in man's nature, and affording a consistent representation of its object, is permanent and alike in all."

Again, we are told that "The idea of God is perfect only when the conditions are complied with"—but, in a majority of cases, "the conditions are not complied with."

Again he says, "The conception of God, as man expresses it, is always imperfect."

And again, "The conception of God is of the most various and evanescent character, and is not the same in any two ages or men."

And again, "The conception which man forms of God depends on his character."

The absurdity of these passages, taken together, is equaled only by other "intuitions" of like character which follow them in the same volume.

First, we are told that the mind of man has three different apprehensions of God, which are spoken of: sentiment, idea, and conception. Now, if we suppose all these to exist at the same time, as this liberal christian evidently does, the notion is a positive absurdity. They might exist consecutively, combined with a doubt which was right; but that they should exist simultaneously as separate apprehensions, is contrary to the laws of mind. If they could exist simultaneously, the one apprehension would nullify the other. One would be various and false, the other permanent and true; while a third would be mysterious and always the same.

But if these succeed each other, which is first, and which is most influential? Mr. Parker tells us that the conception of God is different in all men, and always imperfect. Does this "conception" obliterate the idea which is given as a fact in man's nature? Of what benefit is a true idea if it be obliterated in all men by a conception which is utterly false? Besides, how can a sentiment, the same in all, and an idea which is a fact given in man's nature, ever be varied or perverted by a conception which is different in all men? This sentiment, idea, and conception is a sort of trinity never before thought of; not a trinity in unity, but a trinity in antagonism existing in the same mind.

If man is conscious of these three different apprehensions of God, either in connection or in succession, why does he not choose one of them? But if the idea is a fact given in his nature, then he can not obliterate from his mind a true knowledge of God. And again, would not the "vagueness" of the sentiment be dissipated by the definiteness of the idea, or the force of the conception?

But we are told "that the idea of God comes of the joint and spontaneous action of reason and the religious sentiment"—action of a sentiment?—and again, "that this vague and indefinite sentiment, combined with ignorance and fear, leads to superstition." And then again, "men can by reason get but an imperfect knowledge from nature;" yet from a vague and mysterious sentiment and imperfect data, a Being of wisdom, power, and love, is derived by the reason.

But strange enough, in immediate connection with this, the idea of God is said to be "a fact given in man's nature, which affords a consistent representation of its object, permanent and alike in all." Thus it is at the same time an intuition, given as a fact in man's nature, permanent and alike in all, while yet it is the result of a rational process, predicated upon a vague sentiment and imperfect data.

But strange again, we are told in the same chapter that this idea, which is permanent and alike in all, "depends upon conditions which, in a majority of cases, are not complied with." How can a fact which is the same in all, depend upon conditions? Or, if the fact be unknown until the conditions are complied with, how can any man rationally comply with the conditions of the unknown? The transcendentalist must solve such difficulties for his friends by intuition. They are without the limits of reason.

But the conception of God, as we have been informed, is very different from either the sentiment or the idea. "It is of the most various and evanescent character, and is not the same in any two ages or men." This conception of God, we are told, "depends on a man's character;" that it is bad or good as a man is bad or good; and that it is "always imperfect." But subsequently we hear something very different of this conception. Our author analyzes it, and finds in the evanescent and imperfect conception, which is never the same in any two men, what he denominates the perfect character of God. He says: "At the end of the analysis what is left? Being—Cause—Knowledge—Love—each with no conceivable limitations. To express it in a word, a Being of infinite power, wisdom, and goodness. Thus, by an analysis of the conception of God, we find in fact, or by implication, just what was given synthetically by the intuition of the reason."

Now, as we were taught that the character of the conception depends on the character of the man, and that it is never the same in any age or in any two men, whose conception has the author analyzed? And if he finds this result in one case, according to his own authority, he will certainly find a different one in every other case. And as conceptions have an objective origin, how can an analysis of a conception give an intuition as its result?

But this is not all the author has to teach on the subject of the divine nature and the divine character. Such vagaries as the following occur further on in the same volume:

"God can not be personal and conscious as Joseph and Peter, and yet impersonal and unconscious as moss," etc.

"God is the substantiality of matter!"

"God is the materiality of matter."

"God is universal being."

This is pantheism run mad. If God is substantial, and material, and universal being, he must be developed into all specialities, such as doves and snakes, eagles and alligators, porcupines and pelicans.

Again, "God is infinite motherliness," and "is immanent in all things."

"The things of nature reflect his image, and make real the conception." Yet the conception, we are told, is of the most various and evanescent character.

Again we are told that "we can only know God through self;" but, strange to say, the contrary of this is likewise true, for we are informed that "there is nothing but self between us and God."

Even these are not the worst passages as specimens of rationalism. There are others in which transcendental verbiage becomes worse than ridiculous. As for example; "Nature, which is the outness of God, favors religion, which is the inness of man; and so God works with us. Heathens knew it many centuries ago."

Now, we affirm that this is not true, and we postulate its antagonism thus: "Conceited reason which is the upness of materialism, favors diluted moonshine, which is the inness of transcendentalism; thus mental charlatanism works with vain minds, and men of discernment knew it years ago." In all the attributes of nonsense, the first paragraph is more than a match for the second one. I am almost ashamed to put such rhodomontade upon paper, but I am more ashamed of my countrymen, who hear and laud it.

There are, likewise, in this book evidences of malignity toward the sacred writers and the orthodox faith, which I am sorry to see, and which give a darker hue to its spirit than that given by conceited or erratic intellect. The writer speaks of the Evangelists as "dull evangelists," who may have thrust their own fancies into the mouth of Jesus; and again he says Christ did not call Peter "a false liar, as he was."

Now that a man can write in this way concerning those whom Jesus called his friends and disciples, and commissioned to be the founders of the Christian Church, and concerning one who willingly atoned for an error by penitence and martyrdom, is an indication of hostility so distinct that it is painful. It may not seem so to the skeptical Unitarians, but it will seem so to every one who is in sympathy with the spirit and principles of Christ and his apostles. It may be said that Christ spoke of Peter as a tempter, and admonished him of his errors. But the language of admonition and rebuke serves a purpose. The language of malignity, when no good end can be subserved by it, is a different thing.

I have written these paragraphs to establish a principle. I have used the book of this prominent writer as the representative of a class of Unitarians. If such men would accept revelation as a guide to their reason, and the example and spirit of Christ as model and impulse in the achievement of all real good for humanity, surely they would be wiser and better men. The men who reject these, and yet profess to teach of God and duty, are necessarily blind leaders of the blind.

CHAPTER II.

VARIATIONS AND CONTRADICTIONS IN THE THEOLOGICAL OPINIONS OF SKEPTICS AND TRANSCENDENTALISTS.

How is it that some men tolerate dogmatic assertion and crude philosophisms in such writers as Carlyle, Emerson, and Parker, while on the same subject they require in others mature and accurate thought? It is possible that in relation to some things, the teachings of Christ may not be fully nor clearly apprehended, even by those who receive and obey His instruction; thoughtfully to examine those teachings is, therefore, lawful and proper. If there be objections to the views of Christians, let them be distinctly and fairly stated, and upright minds will hear and weigh the reasons alleged by objectors. If men have a better system to propound, let them show it, and old errors will vanish in the light of a newly-developed truth. Let those who do not discriminate between good sense and pompous pretense, stand agape in the presence of theological bravado and assertion; but will intelligent men accept crude dicta from any one on a subject of serious moment, and accept it with little or no examination?

We do not design in thus writing, to disparage the conceded ability of the authors to whom we have alluded. In some respects they are able and learned men; and the author of this book seems to me to have been sincerely engaged in some of the reform efforts of our time. But any mind, even that of Laplace or Bishop Butler, were it afloat on the sea of skeptical conjecture, without the pole-star by which reason might direct her course, would become perplexed, and would perplex others by its erratic wanderings on a starless sea. Note, therefore, whether there be any evidence of crude and contradictory thought in the teachings of the popular writer already named:—

The author affirms that "Christianity is the absolute religion," and that Jesus taught absolute religion to men. Now this is obviously true, and when rightly considered, it is absolute evidence, not only of the Divine origin, but of the Divine nature of Christianity. Christianity teaches absolute obedience to God. It reveals infinite love in Christ. Love can reach an expression no higher than is given in the crucifixion. It is in Christ stronger than death, hence it is absolute. The Fatherhood of God, the brotherhood of men are taught in ultimate and absolute terms. Filial obedience becomes absolute when we love God with all our heart; and righteousness is absolute when we love our neighbor as ourself. There can be nothing different, nothing better, nothing further in morals and piety than the example and teachings of Christ: hence Christianity, as expressed by the life and teachings of Jesus, is absolute and ultimate religion.

We may affirm that Christianity is absolute in another sense. It is perfectly, and alone, adapted to promote the highest good of men. If received and obeyed in the spirit of its Author, it combines as much of happiness and active usefulness in the life of its recipient as his constitution will permit. Let it be allowed, then, in the accepted sense, that Jesus taught the absolute religion. In this, the true Christian rejoices. This the writer affirms; but yet, as we shall see, he makes his own statement both nugatory and ridiculous. He says in the beginning of his book, that "the religious sentiment does not itself disclose the character, and still less the nature and essence of the object on which it depends."

Again, "The sentiment of God, though vague and mysterious, is always the same in itself." Further on, we are told that "Christianity can be no greater than the religious sentiment, though it may be less." The absolute religion of this rationalist, is no greater than a vague sentiment that does not itself disclose the character of God—"and it may be less." Verily, liberal disciples are in the way of getting a queer idea of "the absolute religion" taught by Jesus.

But furthermore, there is not only one, but there are several judges to aid in deciding that "Christianity is the absolute religion."

We are informed that "Christianity is to be judged of by the religious sentiment—by other forms of religion, and by reason." Strange enough, this—a religion to be judged by a vague sentiment that does not give the character of God! Christianity does give the character of God. How shall it be judged by a sentiment that does not? How shall facts be judged by a sentiment? But the writer's absolute religion is not only to be judged by reason, which is well enough if he means enlightened reason, but it is to be judged by other religions. We supposed the absolute was the judge of all else; but all else is said to judge the absolute.

We are told, again, of a peculiarity of the absolute religion which it is said Jesus of Nazareth taught. He says of Christianity:

"It is not a system of theological or moral doctrines, but a method of religion and life. It lays down no positive creed to be believed in—commands no positive action to be done. It would make man perfectly obedient to God, leaving his thoughts and actions for reason and conscience to govern."

We have, then, an absolute Christianity which is a method without theological or moral doctrines. What does the writer intend to do with his theological doctrine of the religious sentiment? He tells us, too, at the close of his book, that he wants "real Christianity, the absolute religion, preached with faith, and applied to life." Faith in what? A doctrine is a rule of faith and practice; but if "Christianity has neither theological or moral doctrine" in it, and requires neither faith nor practice, how can it be preached with faith?—how applied to life? Does not Mr. P.

mean a transcendental rather than an absolute religion. We think this must be so, as the same author teaches in another volume, that a man may be religious and not know it.

Mr. P. tells us that his absolute religion is a "method of life according to conscience and reason." But a man's conscience is as his faith; and we are told that the absolute religion of Mr. Parker prescribes no creed to be believed. The method, then, must be very various; and it can not be a method of any particular value, for our liberal philosopher tells us, in another place, that "many a savage, his hands smeared all over with human sacrifices, shall come from the east and the west, and sit down in the kingdom of God, with Moses and Zoroaster, with Socrates and Jesus." The worst method in the world, then, will answer the same end as this writer's method. And then we are told that method is all there is of Christianity! O, shame, transcendentalists!

Our author's "absolute Christianity," then, is a religion no greater, but which may be less, than a vague religious sentiment. It offers nothing to be believed. It commands nothing to be done. It is a method of life; but any other method, even a human sacrifice, will answer the same end!

There are other definitions of "absolute Christianity," some of which are better than the foregoing. It would be wrong to pass them without notice. In one place we are told, religion is "perfect obedience to the law of God, revealed in instinct, reason, conscience, and the religious sentiment." The Mormons have this phase of the absolute, putting instinct first, as Mr. Parker does.

There is another definition which approaches the circle of sense, and if the author would accept that "faith which works by love," his definition on this page might be accepted. He says, "Absolute religion is perfect obedience to the law of God"—"perfect love toward God and man exhibited in a life allowing and demanding a harmonious action of all man's faculties so far as they act at all." This is orthodox, and it is a true saying though a little blind as to its import. This is a very different thing from the absolute religion on another page, which proposes nothing to be believed, and requires nothing to be done.

Then again, we have something just the opposite of what is said before. We are told that "Christianity differs from other religions in its eminently practical character." Agreed, my dear sir; eminently practical, certainly, if we take the life and teachings of Christ as its exponent. Let us forget the falsehood and folly of "nothing to be believed and nothing commanded," and listen to the voice of the Master calling us to faith and duty—"Go ye, therefore, teach all nations, baptizing them in the name of the Father, and of the Son, and of the Holy Ghost; teaching them to observe all things whatsoever I have commanded you, and lo! I am with you always, even to the end of the world, Amen."

How different the intent, the thought, and the spirit of this commission from the theological vagaries over which we have passed! Here we have the doctrine of the Trinity—one name, yet three persons in that one name; men to be baptized into that tri-personal name, and taught to "observe all things that Christ had commanded," with the promise annexed of the spiritual presence of Jesus: "Lo! I am with you always, even unto the end of the world."

What is this? Christ, a man like his disciples, and yet to be with them, everywhere and always, unto the end of the world!

CHAPTER III.

LITERARY, MYSTICAL, AND EVANGELICAL ASPECTS OF LIBERAL CHRISTIANITY.

With the exception of Germany, there is, perhaps, no country in the world where students are confined to the study of ideas in text books so long and so intensely, as in America—more especially in the New England States. A boy of five or six years old enters the graded schools of our cities, and villages, and graduates with about as good an education as the English dissenters give their sons, when they are considered fitted for any of the trades or professions. I happen to know from actual observation, that an education which fits a young man for the university in the dissenting schools of England, is generally but little better, in the average of study, than that possessed by the graduate from the graded common schools of our country.

But the New England boy, after he graduates from the people's college, often enters other institutions which give what is called a liberal education. Here he spends five or six years more, a considerable portion of the time in the study of dead languages, in which he sees the ideas of the author, as the blind man saw "trees walking." Not because the dead languages are at fault, but because the subtle shades of thought, often represented by adjuncts, and forms of a sentence, can not be clearly conveyed by a translation. The young man translates and approximates the sense of the passage, and learns to be satisfied with phrases composed of words that have no precise import. Thus he learns to use his own language in involved sentences, which sometimes have a very vague and undetermined sense. The body of the sentence is pretentious, but the soul is vapid or volatile; As in the Dunciad—

"He writes about a thing till all men doubt it,
And writes about it, goddess, and about it."

After his collegiate course the same student often goes to a professional school and spends two or three additional years, when his mind is considered by the recluse professors as fully disciplined, and his education complete:—complete in the same sense that a man who understands the book of Oliver Evans which contains the perfect theory of a grist mill, becomes thereby a practical mill-wright. Such men are often educated out of unison with practical ideas, and out of sympathy with the common sense of the people.

Such statesmen, lecturers, and preachers, are not uncommon in this country, and occasionally make their appearance in Europe. The light of their thought is the glint of the prolonged gossamer, not the sheen of the solid gold. We have had occasion to test the difference between the thought of a self-educated, practical mind, and some of the best minds of the class above referred to. In the political campaign preceding the second election of Abraham Lincoln, it became my business to canvass the senatorial district in which I reside, in behalf of Lincoln and Johnson. I read, of course, the speeches of prominent men on the situation of affairs, and the questions at issue in the campaign:—among others, some of the elaborate speeches of Charles Sumner. Ten sentences would usually express all that could be made of practical use in a half-hour speech of the classic senator, while in a speech of Colfax, there were not ten sentences that could be omitted; and the sententious utterance of Abraham Lincoln, that "it is always dangerous to swap horses while crossing a stream," had more efficacy in determining the minds of enquiring voters in that election, than all the declamation and rhetoric of men whose principles might be right, but whose method of dealing with impending issues were utopian or impracticable.

I do not, as you know, say these things to disparage learning, but to indicate the intrinsically valueless character of rhetorical disquisitions in regard to the good of men; and more especially in regard to such subjects as relate to the religion of Jesus Christ.

This class of men almost necessarily misconceive the character of Jesus, and the redemption from sin which His religion offers to men. They project, from their own plane of thought, a character for the Messiah that suits themselves, and they do not seem to see that the ideal creation of their fancy could never save men from sin. Jesus of Nazareth was a carpenter's son. He was, no doubt, skilled in useful labor. His body was compacted, not by dumb bells or gymnastic exercises, but by manual labor, prompted by an intelligent and worthy motive. His mind was informed and disciplined, not by books only, but by contact with men and things in the actual and practical movements of life. The world and the church will, in the end, learn by the operation of free schools and free labor, that discipline of body as well as of mind is in order to the best and most useful production of thought. There is bright thought that is light thought, (useful in its place;) and good thought that is crude thought; and transcendental thought that is *nonsendental* thought. Such minds will always fail to compass fully even the temporal aims of the Redeemer; much less can they appreciate the spiritual import of His work.

No man can get the right conception of Jesus or His gospel, while he labors to elevate himself in the estimation of his fellow men, rather than to engage in labors to bring his fellow men up towards his own sphere of knowledge and love. Hear the Christian philosopher of Tarsus, learned in the schools and in tent making—"Where is the wise? Where is the scribe? Where is the disputer of this world? Hath not God made foolish the wisdom of this world?"

No such writer as the elegant and learned

Rousseau can understand Christ, nor can any such as the pretentious writers of the transcendental school. "No man can call Jesus, Lord, but by the Holy Ghost." Even His disciples did not fully know Him as a spiritual Messiah until after the resurrection. How, therefore, can those know Him who believe in no resurrection? His lordship is over the spirit of men. His redemption, that of the soul from sin. His religion, that which binds the present to the future life. His sacrifice, to meet a spiritual want, not an intellectual deduction. The profoundest philosophy—meaning thereby the deepest insight into the nature and wants of the soul, will, in the end, declare Jesus to be the revelation of what God is, and what man should be. But the phosphorescent light of vain philosophy, or rather the philosophy of vain pretentious minds, can never attain unto a true knowledge of Christ.

Such writers as Mr. Emerson will always have admirers. There is often eloquence, and beauty, and poetry in their speech. Such writers as Thoreau paint nature in moonlight—sometimes in diluted moonlight. It would be injustice to expect from this class of writers logical deduction, or discriminating analysis. Their gifted muse lives apart from the matter-of-fact things of life and death. Until such writers become little children—which is more difficult than it is for a rich man to enter into the kingdom of heaven—they can neither judge of the spiritual or the natural, as revealed in Jesus.

A friend of the writer selected the following from the morning Daily Register, of London, as rich specimens of the wealth of the transcendental mind. The critic was evidently disposed to see the fallacies and vagaries, rather than the excellencies in Mr. Emerson. We give them with the critique, as illustrative of preceding statements. He says:

"Some disciple of the Atlantic school has selected from Emerson's Conduct of Life, the following passages, which he calls nuggets of gold. If these nuggets are specimens from the mine, we doubt about its being a rich one. Let us analyze some of them, and see if they are not pyrites. Here are some of the nuggets."

"It is the privilege of any human work that is well done, to invest the doer with a certain haughtiness. He can well afford not to conciliate, whose faithful work will answer for him."

'This is both weak and wicked, and contrary to

the maxims of the wise and good in all ages. When a human work is well done, it will not produce a "certain haughtiness" in the mind of any but a fool. Humility is the constant attendant of true greatness. Haughtiness produces evil in the haughty mind, and is offensive and injurious to others.'

"People seem not to see that their opinion of the world is also a confession of character. We can only see what we are, and if we misbehave we suspect others."

'If this be true, then Christ, and all men, both good and evil, who have given a different opinion, are untrue. The Savior and the good in all ages 'have confessed' a very bad character according to this nugget.'

"Why should I hasten to solve every riddle which life offers me? I am well assured that the Questioner, which brings me so many problems, will bring the answers also in due time."

'Will he? Well, let the disciples of the philosopher sit down and wait. In 'due time' they will become the wisest of men.'

"The same correspondence that is between thirst in the stomach, and water in the spring, exists between the whole of man and the whole of nature."

'Very likely! The whole of nature is a very 'large subject'—and as man is a 'part of the whole, whose body nature is, and God the soul,' there will be the same correspondence between him and nature that there is between thirst in the stomach and water in the spring. So far as this is correct, it could be affirmed just as truly of a goose, as of a man.'

"No secret can be kept in the civilized world. Society is a masked ball, where every one hides his real character and reveals it by hiding."

'Well, this is a new discovery. Those that try to keep secrets thereby reveal them. If 'no secret can be kept in the civilized world,' we shall know each other perfectly, hereafter. Nobody can be deceived! What arrant nonsense!'

"Novels are as useful as Bibles, if they teach you the secret that the best of life is conversation, and the greatest success is confidence, or perfect understanding between sincere people."

'Novels are better than Bibles for this purpose. The Bible certainly does not teach this secret. It was both made and revealed by this new teacher of the 'Conduct of Life.''

"A man begins life by trying to prevent men

from cheating him, and ends by ceasing to cheat them."

'If this be true, we have got rid of all the old rogues. And besides, the old maxim regarding the difficulty which once was supposed to exist in regard to the Ethiopian changing his skin, has been overcome. Shame on the men who keep their mouths open, to swallow such pretentious nonsense."

There may be as much of conceited intellect in these criticisms as in the sentences themselves; but they serve to reveal the vapid character of the aliment served and accepted by literary circles of the "radical liberal," or "broad church" men of the East.

I am told that Unitarians, and the liberal and radical religionists of New England, are mostly the admiring readers of Emerson and other *moonsendentalists.* Ought not enquirers of sound sense to find in this fact a subject of reflection?

Mr. Emerson's article in the North American Review on "Originality in Literature," the London Review notices, and after showing that his remarks about Coleridge as a writer are utterly farcical and untruthful, the burden of the article is quoted and noticed, as follows:—

"In making out his case, Mr. Emerson does not embarrass himself much by studying the genealogical tree of a notion, although he can not resist the temptation of bringing Plato and Baron Munchausen together. This sort of exercise belongs to the order of inquiry, which institutes a search after things not generally known. But there is one amazing inconsistency in the article. After we have read of the 'assimilating power,' and begin to understand that genius is fed, and requires to be fed, that it can not intellectually survive on air, and that it must necessarily be indebted, as every thing on this earth is indebted to its surroundings, we come across such a sentence as this, a Bulwerian sentence, ornamented with capital letters: 'The divine resides in the new. The divine never quotes, but is, and creates. The profound apprehension of the Present is Genius, which makes the Past forgotten.' We don't know what the 'divine' is here, and as for the conundrum hidden between the two large Ps of Past and Present, it must be given up; but if there is a gleam of sense, in the passage, it discloses an idea altogether inconsistent with what follows; 'Genius is in the first instance, sensibility, the capacity of receiving just impressions from the external world, and the power of coordinating these after the laws of thought.' This is a clear and a fine definition, (not of genius, but of common sense,) but does it not extinguish that word create? Mr. Emerson knows well that we have nothing to do with creating, that the phrase is loosely and absurdly used; he knows it so well, that he writes this essay in point of fact to prove that 'assimilation' is all we can justly speak of, and yet he must jar the whole tone of a harmonious and symmetrical essay, in order to introduce a characteristic flourish of grand nonsense."

Now is it possible for such minds to understand Jesus of Nazareth? Can the writer of such platitudes understand the Teacher of the beatitudes? A Messiah projected from such minds would be a fantastic philosophist that dies with his generation, not the author of a life-giving faith. "The first Adam was of the earth, earthy, the second Adam is the Lord from heaven."

No man of common sense can believe that philosophers of this school can understand Christ, or believe in Him. Renan, as a historian, occupies a place for fairness and learning far in advance of the host of skeptical writers of the school to which he belongs. In the province of history, as written by Mark and Matthew, not by John, he is eminent; but the spiritual nature of Christ's work, such men can not compass. A man who reads the second chapter of first Corinthians, must either believe that such minds can not understand Christ, or that Paul did not understand Him. After reading such portions of the scripture, one would think that the eagerness of the world to hear what such writers say about Christ, would appear absurdly foolish even to themselves. Paul, holy and profound, learned, and earnest, affirms, as do the other sacred writers, that the "saving health" of the gospel is in its spirit, not in its letter. "The letter killeth but the spirit giveth life." The gospel is a prescription for the spiritual wants and moral diseases of men. Surely, a man may write a history of the physician, who neither understands the elements, nor the effects of his medicine.

It is not pleasant to write thus of a class of men, inspired men, in transcendental phrase, many of whom, in certain connections, have spoken well and truly of Christianity. We wish to render them the respect which is their due—

the same respect that we render to the man who places the works of artists in his mansion, to reveal to others his wealth and his taste, beside the man who takes the orphan from indigence to his home, and sets in a frame of comely apparel, the living lineaments of a picture which art can only imitate. He has the living picture, beautified in mind and body, not for the eye of others, but for love to human souls. Both classes have their merit and reward. One is a christian of the church of society, where "the poor have not the gospel preached unto them;" or they are reformers of the rhetorical school; or those who take christian newspapers to read advertisements of fashionable jewelry, and sermons of gifted preachers, on subjects that sap the foundations, but which never convicted any one of sin. The other is a christian such as was Oberlin, and the Countess of Huntington, William Penn, Arthur Tappan, C. G. Finney, and thousands of kindred hearts in the church of God.

I would by no means disparage the beauties of art. In hours of rest, during an earnest life, I have often lingered in the galleries where the art-gems of the world have been collected. I have two sweet faces that always seem to look on me; one the memorial of a pure hearted child now in heaven, the other of one now living; both were pictures which God had painted in the rough; we took them home to develop their capacities and beauties in our sight, and for His glory. I am sorry for the christian who talks of pictures, and yet places no living ones in his parlors.

Jesus does not discourage delicacy, taste, or amusements that promote human comfort or innocent enjoyment. His mode of life and apparel—His sympathizing with her who brought the precious ointment—His rejoicing with those who rejoiced at the marriage feast, indicate that no one should despise the innocent pleasures of sense, derived from natural objects; but the men and women of the upper vulgar society, deformed by fashion, and paganized with jewels, are no more like the gospel pictures of the good Samaritan, and the woman of the "meek and quiet spirit, whose adorning was not that of wearing of gold, and putting on of apparel," than Hyperion is like a satyr.

Transcendentalism does for the strong mind, what fashion does for a weak mind; only one manifests itself in the intellect, the other in the person. Not only prose, but poetry of cultured minds, loses conscience by lack of faith. John G. Whittier has, no doubt, dwelt with delight on the sweet passages in some of Longfellow's shorter poems; but for all the world, I venture to say, he would not be the author of a poem, untrue in imagery, and utterly devoid of moral and music. Nor would he eviscerate the offspring of his own brain to propitiate either Mammon or Moloch. And the popular preachers and writers, whether transcendental or evangelical, who are in this category, are merely the auctioneers of Vanity Fair.

CHAPTER IV.

BETTER PHASES OF LIBERAL CHRISTIANITY.

We turn now a moment from this seeming digression to a better phase of liberal christianity; to one which gives assurance of a better future for the evangelical side of the Unitarian denomination. I have before me, the most recent statement of this class of liberal christians, in the able and valuable book of James Freeman Clark, of Boston,—"The Truth and Errors of Orthodoxy." There are so many things in this book that fall within the circle prescribed by a true faith, and so many things by which all parties might learn charity, and a better phraseology in announcing their doctrines, that I hesitate to make needful strictures, and would prefer leaving the author and his party to follow the impulse which they seem to have, to make progress in the right direction. I shall speak, therefore, in regard to the failures of the volume as shortcomings, rather than fallacies—some of them as indices pointing in the direction of that saving faith, which "works by love and purifies the heart."

There are some things said among the many, in regard to inspiration, that are well and truly written. There are some things in regard to the verbal and equal inspiration of the books of the Old Testament especially, which will do good, But there is failure to reach the truth in regard to the New Testament, as an ultimate and perfect dispensation, and in regard to the perfect instruction and authority of the apostolic writings. This is a failure that necessarily injures progress in holiness, just so far as it impairs confidence in the New Testament, as truth from God.

The author speaks, as transcendentalists do, of the intellectual gifts of distinguished men, as a species of inspiration. This expanding of the definition, darkens counsel, and is in itself a misnomer, because those who use it would refuse to apply it to the great intellects of malefactors, and artists of evil, who have appeared in the world.

After making a clear discrimination in such

words as, "the source of the one inspiration is the works of nature, the source of the other, the inward Christ;" the writer in parts of his discussion has such sentences as the following: "The writers of the New Testament had no different inspiration from that of all other christians."

"Christ does not say that those who are to write the gospels or the epistles, shall be guarded against all possible error."

"The writers of the Bible no where claim that they were inspired to write these books."

Again, the author admits that authority is necessary in order to the efficacy of truth, but the chief authority he gives to the truth of the New Testament teachers, is their better knowledge of the facts: The self-evidencing nature of truth itself, apart from its authorship, and the testimony of the church in all ages, that the inspired writings are profitable for instruction in righteousness.

Now, as we shall see, the author's statements on these subjects taken together, fail to come up either to the requirements of reason, or the statements of scripture. It is a self-evident proposition that if the New Testament dispensation is from God, it will be adapted perfectly to accomplish its end. But no specific end can be accomplished by truth, unless that truth is fitted in itself when applied to the human soul, to produce the end sought. No matter what we may conceive that end to be, a development of holiness in individual minds and in the world, as stated in the scriptures, or some other end; if God be the author of the dispensation, the means would be adapted to accomplish the divine design. To suppose that perfect love and obedience could be achieved by an imperfect revelation of truth, is the height of unreason.

The inspiration of the New Testament may adapt truth to minds of different temperaments, different degrees of knowledge, and to different degrees of advancement in the same mind. Indeed, this would be necessary in a system of inspiration. It may even be necessary that there should be passages which contain no saving truth; and passages so presented as to try the intellect and the heart, especially the vain intellect, and the foolish heart. There should be problems and parables as well as precepts and principles in a system of inspiration: some open now, others to be progressively opened in the future; but that God would give authority to truth not perfectly adapted to accomplish His end is preposterous.

The inspiration of Jesus would be of no value to the world, if the writers of the New Testament were not guides to a correct presentation of His thoughts, and to that interpretation of them that would accomplish good both present and future. In the gospel of the Hebrews it is written, "God hath in these last days spoken unto us by His Son." But what God has said through His Son, we hear only in the words of the apostles. This is according to the Savior's express appointment and design. Immediately before His ascension into the spiritual world He said, "Ye shall receive power after that the Holy Ghost is come upon you; and ye shall be witnesses unto me, both in Jerusalem and in all Judea, and in Samaria, and unto the uttermost part of the earth." Did not these witnesses tell "the truth, the whole truth, and nothing but the truth?"

It is so far from being the whole truth that the apostles do not claim inspiration, in any other sense than that of possessing the gifts of the Spirit common to all true believers, that

Jesus especially declares that they were selected not only to be His witnesses, because they had been with Him from the beginning; but that the especial end for which they were chosen and ordained, was that they might transmit His doctrines to the future; and He adds the promise, that in order to do this, His words should be brought supernaturally to their memory. The words of Christ on this subject are so plain that it is passing strange that writers, not only liberal, but evangelical, should have so long failed to discern the import of the statement.

Jesus says to His disciples when about to leave them in the world, "Henceforth I call you not servants, for the servant knoweth not what his Lord doeth, but I have called you friends, for all things that I have heard of my Father, I have made known unto you. Ye have not chosen me, but I have chosen you, and ordained you, that ye should go and bring forth fruit, and that your fruit should remain." That is, the truth of the dispensation was communicated to them, not as the common servants of Christ, but as friends who had learned all things from the Father by the Son, that they might use their knowledge for His glory. The Holy Spirit inspired holy thought, while providence furnished the historic medium. One is the body, the other the soul.

Jesus chose and ordained the disciples in a peculiar sense, not true of others. For what purpose? That they should go and bring forth fruit, and that their fruit should remain. Now this fruit can mean nothing else than the institutions they should establish, and the gospels and epistles they should write. Hence the work and words of the apostles remain in the churches, and will remain forever. Christ beyond controversy speaks of the truths that He communicated to them. This is enough for us to know. "He that hath ears to hear, let him hear what the Spirit says to the churches."

Not only this, but the promises annexed to their commission are so explicit that it is difficult to misapprehend their import. It was promised of the Holy Spirit, who came in the name of Christ, and who was the spiritual Christ after the Pentecost: "He shall guide you into all truth,"—"He shall bring all things to your remembrance whatsoever I have told you." "He shall show you things to come." "When the Comforter is come, whom I will send unto you from the Father, even the Spirit of Truth, which proceedeth from the Father, He shall testify of me, and ye shall bear witness because ye have been with me from the beginning." This is clearly and designedly inspiration beyond that of common christians. This is all the friends of a divine revelation need to claim. Truth, impulse, and guidance from God, for all ages of the church till the end of time.

It is scarcely necessary to add, that the apostles themselves were conscious of divine guidance in communicating the truth. In the first letter to the Corinthians, Paul says, "Now we have received not the spirit of the world, but the Spirit which is of God, that we might know the things that are freely given us of God; which things also we speak, not in the words which man's wisdom teacheth, but which the Holy Ghost teacheth." And Peter in his second letter—"Be mindful of the words which were spoken before by the holy prophets, and of the commandments of us, the apostles of the Lord and Savior."

Whatever, therefore, may be said by learned men concerning parts of the Old Testament, and passages of the New, there can be no reasonable doubt about the inspiration of the christian Scriptures, and the adaptation of inspired truth to the sanctification of the human soul. Jesus Christ Himself affirmed this when He prayed, "Sanctify them through Thy truth: Thy word is truth."

There is, likewise, a failure in this best book which the Unitarians have produced, to perceive the nature and kind of authority which truth must have in order to save the soul from sin. The authority ascribed to truth by the author, would be utterly inadequate to give it saving power. The glory of the gospel is not mostly in its precept; it is in its manifestation of the character and love of the God-head; and in the spiritual power granted by faith to enable men to feel, to will, and to do what they know to be duty. What men need is not more light, but a disposition to do the good they know.

Seneca lived with Paul both in time and place. His morals are pure, and commend themselves to men by their intrinsic worth. The Romans believed Seneca and grew worse; while whoever among the same people believed Paul, grew better. The conscience will enforce no truth upon the soul, however perfect, unless it sees the authority of God in it. So we are made. Faith has eyes, but she can not see in the dark. Without revelation she becomes a blind leader of the blind. And when conscience is palsied by no faith, or corrupted by a false one, it is a sleeping sentinel, or it is a blind giant, enforcing error upon the soul. Truth then must have the light of God to guide Faith, and the authority of God to empower the conscience; then "he that believeth shall be saved."

The Redeemer of the world did not rely upon His own truth, with all its internal and external authority, to sanctify men, until the direct authority of God, and the influence of the Spirit were superadded. He referred His disciples to His approaching resurrection from the dead, as the divine authorization of His truth. He was "declared to be the Son of God with power, by the resurrection from the dead." This divine sanction was the authority which they should use, and which the Holy Spirit would use in the work of salvation. In His last conversation with His appointed apostles, He promised that He would send the Comforter into the world—"And when He is come, He will reprove the world of sin, of righteousness, and of judgment.

Of sin, because they believe not on me; of righteousness, because I go to the Father, and of judgment, because the prince of this world is judged." "I have many things to say unto you, but ye can not bear them now. Howbeit, when He, the Spirit of Truth is come, He will guide you into all truth."

After the resurrection, the truth that He taught, and which had been neglected as mere human precept, would be recognized as authorized of God, and become the standard of righteousness by which men would judge themselves, and by which God would judge them. The words of the apostles, as His commissioned witnesses, would then accomplish more than the words of Jesus Himself did before the resurrection. As He said, "The works which I do ye shall do, and greater works shall ye do, because I go to my Father."

In almost every chapter of this volume of Dr. Clarke, relating to the essential things of salvation, we might note what we consider to be a failure to perceive, or to state fully the doctrines of the New Testament. Concerning the doctrine of Christ's sacrifice, there are words of appreciation, which, were they sustained by the subsequent exhibition of the subject, would be gratifying to all believers in Jesus. But the statements that fall within the circle of saving doctrine, may be lost to the readers of the book, by reason of the abatement, or misdirection which other passages give them. And yet to truth-loving readers of the New Testament, this abatement we hope will often fail of effect. The comparison of the sacrifice of Christ, which Dr. Clarke declares, was "a real and true sin-offering," convincing us of the evil of sin, and the love of God, with the martyrdom of good men in past ages, will have little influence with thoughtful enquirers. No one reading the scriptures, enquiring what they must do to be saved, will fail to perceive significance, and a deep relation to sin and salvation in Christ's suffering, which have no parallel or approximation in human history.

In the summing up of the author, he says: "We can believe that God in Christ does reconcile the world to himself." The scriptures says, "God was in Christ, reconciling the world to himself,"—"does create a sense of pardoned sin,"—in those who repent and believe in the Lord Jesus Christ, should be added; "does remove the weight of transgression,"—there should be added; in the case of those who love Christ, and have ceased consciously to disobey him;— "does take away the obstacle in our conscience," not till the soul has the sense of pardon by entire submission to Christ;—"does help us to a living faith, hope, peace and joy,"—these are the fruits of the spirit in the soul, which no man ever did, or ever will experience, except he sees the love of God in Christ, and is conscious of obedience. No man ought to make general, what God has made special. The only hope of the soul is, that "the blood of Christ, who through the Eternal Spirit, offered himself without spot unto God, shall purge the conscience from dead works, to serve the Living God." The pronouns as Jesus and the apostles spoke them, refer to those who have faith, not to mankind in general.

We notice only another instance; and this because it is depended upon with apparent confidence by the author, to prove that the apostles were not inspired in the sense in which their teaching is received by evangelical christians. It is affirmed that the apostles "were mistaken in regard to the time of Christ's second appearing." Now, it is only a half truth that they expected or hoped that Christ would come during their own age. The time of His coming was indefinite in their minds, and designed by the author of inspiration to be so. Jesus taught them distinctly, in various connections, that the time of His coming at the end of the dispensation, "was not for them to know." Instead of this, they were to watch at all times, and be ready for the event. In words which left a deep impression, He taught them that this was the only proper state of mind in regard to "the end of the world." We can now see many reasons to believe that if inspiration had given them, or any one, the time of the end, it would have been an injury, not a benefit. The motive drawn from approaching death, or the end of the world, has not the exhilaration, hope and joy in it, that the appearing of the Lord in His kingdom and glory, will always have for the believer. How it is I know not; but I could rejoice with all my heart, if I were sure that Christ would come this year. But I would not so rejoice in the assurance of my own death within the same time.

To allege, as an argument against their inspiration, that they did not know a point in the time of future events, that the Master taught them it was not best they should know, is surely a misapprehension of the nature of the case.

When the disciples asked Jesus the three questions in Matthew 24th—the signs of the destruction of the temple—His coming to establish the gospel dispensation—and of the end of the world, He tells them the signs which will precede the two first, which should occur before the death of some then present; but in regard to the last question, the end of the world, he affirms: "But of that day and that hour knoweth no man, no, not the angels of heaven, but my Father only. Watch therefore, for ye know not what hour your Lord doth come."

This was the doctrine taught by Jesus; ye are not to know the time when the New Testament age will end; be ye therefore always ready. He taught them farther, however, that before His coming, a probation would intervene, at the end of which, each of them would have to give an account of the use he had made of his talent, and be judged accordingly. He had likewise spoken to them of an apostacy that would occur before the final issue; and as Peter informs us, He had promised another geological transformation, or reconstruction of the earth, after which, those saved from the old condition, were to be the glorified denizens of the "new heavens and new earth, in which dwelleth righteousness.

Besides, the hope of the first age was true, because if the Lord did not come to them, they came to the Lord at the close of their own probation; and if Dr. Clarke's views of the resurrection be correct, we see not how he can hold his own views and speak of the hope of Christ's second coming as a mistake.

But the apostles did not favor the views of some in the early churches, that Christ's personal appearance was immediately impending. Paul writes to the church at Thessalonica, which was unduly agitated on this subject, and teaches expressly, that before the second coming of Christ there would be a great apostacy which had already begun to manifest itself. He then gives a distinct description of the Papal superstition, marking the character of the Roman apostacy for us and for them. For them, that they might know the "man of sin" had not yet come; for us, that we might know when He should come.

No man can read this description understandingly, without seeing the spirit of prophecy and of inspiration, pointing to the Papal power as the culmination of an apostacy to intervene before the second coming of Christ. Here are the passages:

Paul had written in the fourth chapter of his first letter to Thessalonica, an urgent exhortation in view of the Lord's appearing, and closes in the beginning of the fifth chapter with the inspired idea of the time; "But of the times and the seasons, brethren, ye have no need that I write unto you; for you, yourselves, know that the day of the Lord so cometh as a thief in the night." This, with other things, had led the Thessalonians to look for an immediate manifestation of Christ. This misapprehension led Paul in his second letter, to speak more distinctly in regard to the event. In the second chapter of second Thessalonians he says, "Now we beseech you brethren, by the coming of our Lord Jesus Christ, and by our gathering together unto Him, that ye be not soon shaken in mind, or be troubled, neither by spirit, nor by word, nor by letter, as from us, as that the day of the Lord is at hand; let no man deceive you by any means;

for that day shall not come, except there come a falling away first, and that man of sin be revealed, the son of perdition who opposeth and exalteth himself above all that is called God, or that is worshipped, so that he, as God, sitteth in the temple of God, showing himself that he is God. Remember ye not, that when I was with you, I told you these things? and now ye know what withholdeth, that he—the man of sin—may be revealed in his time. For the mystery of iniquity doth already work, only he that now restraineth will continue, until he be taken out of the way; and then that wicked power will be revealed, whom the Lord shall consume with the spirit of His mouth, and destroy with the brightness of His coming. Even Him, whose coming is after the workings of Satan, with all power, and signs, and lying wonders."

In his first letter to Timothy, this apostle also speaks of the same apostacy, and adds two other characteristics. He says "Now the spirit speaketh expressly that in the latter times some shall depart from the faith, giving heed to seducing spirits and doctrines of demons, (i. e. spirits of the dead,) * * forbidding to marry, and commanding to abstain from meat," as the Church of Rome does.

The apostle Peter, likewise, in his second letter, writing on this absorbing subject, reveals further the apostolic consciousness in regard to it for his own time, and for ours. He tells them in the fourth chapter, that "There shall come in the last days, scoffers, walking after their own lusts, and saying—'Where is the promise of His coming; for since the Fathers fell asleep, all things continue as they were from the beginning of the creation."' This refers to the atheistic philosophy prevalent in those days and in ours, that God started the machinery of the universe, and then withdrew Himself, or fell asleep, leaving every thing to be governed thenceforth by inexorable law.

Peter replied to such scoffers precisely as we do now; referring to the geological changes of the past, and those that in the order of mundane and moral progress must come in the future; he then adds—"But the day of the Lord will come as a thief in the night, in the which the heavens shall pass away with a great noise, and the elements shall melt with fervent heat; the earth also, and the works that are therein shall be burned up." * * Nevertheless, we, according to His promise, look for "new heavens and a new earth wherein dwelleth righteousness." "Wherefore beloved, seeing ye look for such things, be diligent that ye may be found of Him without spot, and blameless."

We have dwelt on this subject more at length, inasmuch as Dr. Clarke has fallen into the error which the infidel class of liberal christians constantly urge, in regard to the "mistake" of the apostles, as they complacently call it, that the Lord was immediately to appear. Surely, the seal of divine inspiration is deeply impressed upon this subject. Inspiration, adapting the truth to their age, and to all ages. While the apostle Paul maintained the injunction to watch and be always ready, he described minutely that Papal apostacy which was to intervene before the Lord should appear. Peter farther refers to the vain and unwise scoffers, who, on scientific grounds, deny divine interposition, and affirm the permanency of all forms and forces since the beginning. These intervening events have been developed, and the christian church stands now at the opening of the seventh seal, looking for the coming of the Lord. "Amen. Even so. Come Lord Jesus."

CHAPTER V.

DEVELOPMENT OF DIVINE REVELATION IN THE THREE DISPENSATIONS OF POWER, LAW, AND LOVE.

The rational and scriptural scheme of the progressive development of Divine Revelation, is, in my opinion, imperfectly apprehended by theological teachers and writers, both Liberal and Evangelical. On this subject, Dr. Clarke has some passages which affirm the advance of truth, and authority of the New Testament compared with the Old; but there is not in his book, nor in any other that I have met with, a discriminating statement of the progressive development of Revelation, and of the connection of the three dispensations of power, law, and love.

A right understanding of this subject will aid in the discussion of the doctrine of inspiration; and present a strong testimony to the reason that the Divine guidance has been over all, in the progressive revealment of the divine character. Conglomerating the three dispensations into one, the immature and introductory Old, with a perfect New, is a fruitful source of superstition and skepticism.

The Old Testament institutions and ordinances were, in some respects, symbolical of the perfect spiritual dispensation that was to follow them. The old dispensations, the Patriarchal and Mosaic, were perfectly adapted to their age and place, in the order of progressive revelation, from less to greater degrees of light and love.

The law of development, i. e., progress from lower to higher forms, forces, and faculties, is the universal law of the divine government over matter and mind.

In the process of creation, the earth has been advanced from lower to higher conditions, the vegetable kingdom from less to more perfect species, or rather from more simple to more compound structures, and the animal kingdom from lower, to higher forms and faculties. These have all been developed progressively, in adaptation to each other; vegetables and animals being constantly advanced in adaptation to the changing conditions of the earth's surface.

There are two opinions held by well-informed men, in regard to the method by which God has accomplished this advance, from the less to the more perfect, in nature. Some hold that the more perfect species, were, in some way, developed out of the less perfect. Others hold that as new conditions are produced on the earth's surface, new and more perfect species are created.

But whatever may be true in regard to the *modus operandi* of the divine working, no one who understands the subject, doubts that God has developed all departments of nature progressively, from lower to higher forms and faculties. The law of progressive development, then, is the mode of the Divine working, in all time and in all departments of nature. This statement is verified not only by scientific evidence, but it is explicitly affirmed in the Bible.

Now what is true in nature, is true likewise in revelation. God has advanced the dispensations from the less to the more perfect. Each of the elder dispensations is perfectly adapted to the darker age in which it was given; but each is imperfect in truth and grace, light and love, when compared with the dispensation of Christ.

Notice—1st. The evidence and the method of the progressive development of revelation.

In the first, or patriarchal dispensation, the moral character of God was very imperfectly known. It was the dispensation of Creation; God was worshiped as Creator—as the Almighty. "Almighty power and Godhead," were the attributes known to worshipers: Little more, probably, than that which can be deduced by reason from the works of creation. By the name JEHOVAH, revealed in the Mosaic dispensation, God was not known to the Patriarchs. In the Patriarchal Dispensation, the family was the center of religious service and culture, and from the family it was developed into the nation.

That which was good and of permanent utility in a previous condition, was not lost by the advance to a better, but it was incorporated with the new knowledge. Hence, the patriarchal was developed into the national, retaining family duties, and the name of God was further revealed from Creator to Lawgiver, but retaining the previous attribute, so that Jehovah was the Almighty Lawgiver; and God was worshiped in the second dispensation both as Almighty Creator and Lawgiver.

The imperfect theology of the Patriarchal dispensation was likewise advanced one stage into that of Moses. Theology in Job's time argued the question whether the Almighty rewarded men on earth according to merit; and Abraham did not know but that the Almighty would accept a human sacrifice of the first-born, a terrible usage prevalent in the early ages among heathen nations, until God, by direct interposition, tried him, and by selecting the sacrifice thereby taught him a better knowledge of his character.

In the Mosaic or Legal Dispensation an advanced development was inaugurated. The family, by a common bondage and suffering, was consolidated into a nation, and the centre of worship made national. A new name of God was revealed, to which the former knowledge of Creator and Almightiness was attached, and the written ritual law was enacted, by which the attributes of justice and mercy were more fully developed. The Creator thus endowed, was enthroned as Almighty, Lawgiver, and Judge of men.

The memorial of the Sabbath day was changed, or rather enlarged to include the advanced light. From being a sacred memorial of the finished work which initiated the Dispensation of Creation, it came to be likewise a memorial of the act which initiated the Dispensation of Law. The Jewish Church, in addition to the first memorial, was commanded to keep the Sabbath in remembrance of the deliverance from Egypt.

The development of the dispensations to the perfect, was symbolized in the Jewish dispensation, and is distinctly taught in the New Testament. The tabernacle had three courts: First, that of the Gentiles, into which all might enter. This was the dispensation of nature, or of Creation, when all worshipers acknowledged the one Almighty Creator, until tradition failed, and was superceded by written languages. The second court, was that of the Jews, into which Jews only could enter, and where the religious ceremonial of the nation was observed. This symbolized the second dispensation. The third court symbolized the Christian dispensation. Into this no Gentile or Jew could yet enter, but the high priest once a year, to offer sacrifice. Paul teaches us that the veil which separated the "holy of holies" from the court of the Jews, signified that the "holiest dispensation of all," the Christian, was not yet accessible. "The old dispensation could not make men perfect, as to their conscience," and the new was not accessible to them. When Christ cried "it is finished" on the cross, this veil in the temple was rent in twain, signifying that the way into the "holiest of all" was accomplished. The development to the perfect was complete by Christ's sacrifice.

The New Testament is the third, and perfect, dispensation, developed from the second—the introductory dispensation of Moses. There were, "first the blade, then the ear, then the ripe corn in the ear"—the "harvest" dispensation of the world-field. The "new wine" of the new dispensation was not to be put into the "old bottles" of the legal dispensation—nor was the new to be attached to the old, as new cloth upon an old garment. The new was in the old, only as the ripe corn was in the immature blade and ear.

The New Testament church was to take heed to the preachers of the old, as to "a light shining in a dark place." The old was a dark dispensation of "types and shadows" that "made nothing perfect," but the prophets were the light of their age. To this light men were to take heed, until the daylight of the gospel rose in their minds. Then, when the gospel truth was written and established, the morning star, which had arisen in their hearts, would sink in the deeper glory of the day-light; and the "light shining in a dark place," would be needed as evidence, but not as guidance.

The dispensation of Moses was a dispensation of law. The moral law of the stone tables, as the law of the Sabbath, was made for man, hence a part of all dispensations. But the ceremonial law and the municipal law of Moses were changeable, and in some respects imperfect, because adapted to the darker age, and the darker minds of men in that age. Deuteronomy, or the second law, changed previous enactments, and changed the penalties for certain crimes, in some cases two or three times. The obvious reason was, that, when the circumstances of the people changed from a nomadic to a settled community, their advanced condition required a change both in statute and penalty. The law of divorce in the old dispensation, would be immoral in the new dispensation. This, and other things, permitted on account of the "dark place," are abrogated and condemned in the light of Christ's teaching and example.

"The law came by Moses, but grace and truth by Jesus Christ." The old law, even if it were perfect in its place, is neither light nor love, in the sense that the New Testament dispensation is such. The first was especially the dispensation of power, the second of law, the third of "love and truth;" the last combining and perfecting the two preceding. The love of the old dispensation was for the temporal deliverance of the nation. The love of Christ is for the spiritual deliverance of the soul.

"Moses was a servant in all his house." Those who lived under the old dispensation, served God as servants do their masters. Under Christ's dispensation it is not servant and master, under law, but son and father—the obedience of love—or better, the obedience by love to the law, as illustrated by the teaching and example of Christ. "The commandment going before was disannulled, because of its weakness and unprofitableness; for the law made nothing perfect, but the bringing in of a better hope did."

With the advanced light of the New Testament, there came likewise an advanced administration of the Holy Spirit. "But if the ministration of death, written and engraven in stones, was glorious, so that the children of Israel could not steadfastly behold the face of Moses, for the glory of his countenance, which glory was to be done away; how shall not the ministration of the Spirit be rather glorious: for if the ministration of condemnation be glory, much more doth the ministration of righteousness exceed in glory; for even that which was made glorious, had no glory in this respect, by reason of the glory that excelleth. For if that which is done away is glorious, much more that which remaineth is glorious."

The Sabbath, under the new dispensation was developed into the spiritual, and retained the physical rest of preceding dispensations. It was changed to commemorate the finished work of Christ, as its capital memorial. The development of the Sabbath as a positive institution, was, first, the finished work of creation; second, the finished work of national deliverance; third the finished work of Christ. A memorial of the complete initiation of each dispensation.

2. Notice now the method and the power by which the progressive development of the three dispensations was accomplished. The character of the object of worship, is that which affects

and transforms the character of the worshiper; by faith, transforming the one into the image of the other, from glory to glory.

The Name of God had a new development in each dispensation, "from faith to faith," first, the Almighty, Alshadi, adoni, elohim, revealed the one Creator, in opposition to polytheism. The chief attributes were those taught by nature, eternal power and Godhead. Under the second dispensation, the new name, Jehovah, was given, and the attributes of justice and mercy, in the lawgiver, were more perfectly revealed. In the third dispensation, the one name of God is revealed in the tri-fold manifestation of Father, Son, and Holy Ghost.

The first manifestation was in nature; the second in symbol and written language; the third in the person of our Lord and Saviour Jesus Christ. To all of these, angelic and supernatural aids were added, sufficient to connect the manifestation of each dispensation with the true God, the Creator.

Thus, as the Name of God was developed, the moral character of the worshipers was developed in accordance with the attributes revealed. The moral character of God being revealed progressively, it develops the moral character of the worshipers progressively in each dispensation, "from faith to faith."

The only principle, which is the same through all the dispensations is faith. Faith, or credence, is the band which connects the power with the machinery. The power is the divine character: the machinery is the faculties of the human mind: faith is the band that unites the two, so that the power of the one operates the other.

Hence faith in God's character, so far as it is revealed, is all God requires of men. And, although in the old dispensations, it could not make men righteous, in the sense of the New Testament, yet "it was imputed to them for righteousness." Abraham, who by faith obeyed up to the amount of his knowledge and ability, was as righteous in the sight of God's requirement, although not as perfect in moral character, as John or Paul.

There was likewise a development in each dispensation in itself, from the less to the more perfect. The dispensation of nature was dark and diabolical in its first stages. Its representative men in its later stages, Job, Abraham, and the Patriarchs, were better men.

The first stages of the Mosaic dispensation were dark, fabulous, and cruel, as exemplified in the judges. The Prophets were sun-crowned men, immensely in advance of the early periods of their dispensation. John Baptist was the last of these, and the greatest of them all, and the greatest born of women, but the least in the Gospel dispensation, is greater than he.

The Christian dispensation after its initiation, was likewise to be developed from lower to higher stages of knowledge and perfection. Not that any thing can be added to, or substracted from, the revealed truth of the New Testament. But, in the words of the immortal Robinson, "increasing knowledge will be derived from the Scriptures," and the light of truth, and the purifying power of love, will prevail more and more in the true churches, until Christ comes at the close ot the dispensation. The great apostacy is to be destroyed by the "light of His coming."

There is another development beyond our dispensation, of which Christ spoke to His disciples, but which is properly, but dimly seen, as the zodiacal light, shedding glory beyond the horizon of the gospel day. "Nevertheless, we, according to his promise, look for a new heaven and a new earth in which dwelleth righteousness."

The earth, which has undergone many advancing transformations in the past, will undergo one in the future, to perfect physical conditions. Then, those, who like Paul, attain unto the resurrection state, or a state in which the soul is so advanced to perfection, as to require in the nature of things, a perfect spiritual body in adaptation to its advanced condition, will, perfect in soul and body, become the denizens of a perfect sphere. And as the perfect can not die, they will live and reign with Christ for ever and ever. "Amen: even so, come Lord Jesus."

The churches of the reformation, need some Paul, as did the churches of the formation, to detach them from the Old Testament as a perfect system, or as being in any wise equal with the New Testament. Except in the elementary articles of the moral law, the marriage covenant, and such other provisions as were made for man in all time, the Old Testament is an immature and introductory dispensation.

There has been constant evil done to the moral interests of men, by making the Old Testament and the New equal in precept and obligation. Servitude existed in a modified form in the darker dispensation. The Dispensation of

Moses greatly modified the Dispensation of Power in regard to servants. But the servitude and polygamy permitted by Moses, are utterly at variance with the truth and love of the new dispensation. The slaves of "believing masters," were freed under the gospel; and even the slaves still "under the yoke," served for Christ's sake, "suffering wrongfully."

Hence, the effort to show that slavery, under the Old Testament, was in any wise applicable to the question under the New, was an error productive of immense evil, both South and North. Erroneous teaching on this subject hindered the progress of reformation both in Europe and in this country.

Such, likewise, is the case with the polygamy of the Old Testament. It is said that a Bible distributor made an effort to supply the Mormons. He was received gladly. They claimed that the Bible justified their practice. The distributor retired, disgusted no doubt, with their heresy; but himself in the dark, so far that his error in appreciating the relations of the two dispensations prevented his correcting their false views of revelation.

Such, likewise, is the case, when Old Testament saints are made examples for New Testament practice. The Old Testament saints, as a general statement, would be New Testament sinners. Some of them, as David, sinned grossly, even in the light of their own dispensation. In that light it was declared by the Lord that the sword should never pass from David's house; and because he was a "man of blood," he was not permitted to build the house of the Lord. The effort to justify Old Testament character by the light of the Gospel, has a baleful effect, in some cases, both upon minister and hearer.

Such teaching makes skeptics, as in the case of the writers of the Westminster Review, and liberal christians. Men must be false to reason enlightened by the Gospel, before they can believe the Old Testament to be the perfect will of God.

CHAPTER VI.

PERSONALITY OF GOD.

The skepticism of our times, like its talented preachers, is popular in many circles of well-informed people. I call it skepticism, because, while it assails the generally received faith of evangelical Christians, it offers no comprehensible system instead of the faith it labors to destroy. It begets doubt, but it produces no conviction that is influential upon the heart and will of men. It is, therefore, skepticism; and if the Christian religion, is a benefit to mankind which all admit, then those who introduce doubt or something worse in its stead, are evil doers.

This skepticism is popular in some instances, because it assumes the attitude of reform, and therefore commends itself to minds of humane and progressive tendencies. It is popular in a wider sense with many who desire to retain the name of Christian while they refuse obedience to Christ. In the name of Jesus it denies the divine authority of Christianity; whether a man receive or reject the gospel, he is a Christian:—he that believeth shall be saved, and he that believeth not shall be saved. Such a system has the elements of popularity in it with all sorts of men, except those who maintain the Scripture doctrine, that repentance and faith in the Lord Jesus Christ are conditions of holiness and therefore of eternal life.

But does this modern phase of skepticism commend itself to the reason of fair-minded men? Should the doubts which it encourages concerning the foundational truths of revealed religion be entertained? Let us put into the balance of reason some of its utterances, and weigh them against the doctrines of the Christian faith.

It is noticeable, that while the writers of the Carlyle school, such as Emerson and Mr. Parker, adopt language which speaks of God as a personal being, they likewise write many passages which make the impression that there is no personal God; or none that can be called personal in any comprehensible sense. On this, as on other subjects of the most grave interest, one may find on one page of their books a distinct recognition of truth, while in another place the same truth is perplexed by doubt, nullified by contradictory expressions, or rendered incomprehensible by words as innocent of any particular import as moonshine is of caloric.

We have noticed, in a preceding letter, the peculiar philosophy in relation to the "idea," "sentiment," and "conception" of God. Now, if any disciples of the liberal school suppose that by this teaching they know any thing about God as a personal being, there are several passages in the same volume that will correct that mistake at once. It had been said that all men have an idea of God; but, according to other passages, if any one believes that he knows any thing about God, either as a personal, or a conscious divine being, or that he has any comprehensible "idea" whatever on this subject, it is all a mistake. Notice this in the following passage in "Discourses of Religion."

"We talk of a personal God. If thereby we only deny that he has the limitations of unconscious matter, no harm is done. But our conception of personality is that of finite personality, limited by human imperfections, hemmed in by time and space, restricted by partial emotions—displeasure, wrath, ignorance, caprice. Can this be said of God? If matter were conscious, as Locke thinks it possible, it must predicate materiality of God, as persons predicate personality. If it mean God has not the limitations of our personality, it is well. But if it mean that he has those of unconscious matter, it is worse than the other term. Can God be personal and conscious as Joseph and Peter—unconscious and impersonal as moss, or the celestial ether? No man will say it. Where, then, is the philosophic value of such terms?" We affirm that this is not only directly contradictory to what was said before, but that there is neither philosophy nor sense in it.

Our author as we have seen, analyzes the conception which he says men form of God, and finds in it "power, wisdom, and love," without limitation. Now, if the idea of personality in God must be limited by human imperfection, why not wisdom and love thus limited? There is contradiction in affirming the one and denying the other. So that, if it is affirmed that God is not personal in any comprehensible sense, then the writer must affirm, according to his own showing, that God is neither wise nor unwise, good nor evil, in any comprehensible sense. To affirm personality of God as an infinite being, is as we shall see, more rational than to affirm wisdom or love of him, because the human idea of moral character, without revelation, is imperfect; but the idea of personal identity is absolute, and always the same in all beings.

There are some things which are the same in themselves, and the same forever. Truth must be the same to all intelligent beings, so far as known to them. Two and three are five with God, as they are with Joseph and Peter. Self-consciousness can not be one thing in God, and another thing in man. The absolute truths of the universe, when known, must be the same to all beings that have a moral nature, or else the moral universe is founded on the principle of discord. Personality is an absolute truth; it is an intuition. We conceive of it in God as distinctly as we know it in ourselves.

The reasons, annexed to the above paragraph, are about equal to the reasons annexed to transcendental statements on some other subjects. So far as there is any reason in the matter, the author's idea is, that because God can not be affirmed to be impersonal and unconscious as the moss and the celestial ether, therefore He is not personal nor conscious. If the argument were good for any thing, then, as two opposite characteristics are instanced in the objects named, instead of proving that God is neither conscious nor unconscious, personal or impersonal, it would prove that He is both the one and the other. The foregoing passage is written in the phrase of blank pantheism.

Furthermore, it is admitted by the writer that man is a personal and conscious being, and that matter is not personal or conscious. It is conceded that personal agents and impersonal objects do exist. To deny this would be to deny the validity of both sense and reason. Now, if it be a fact that personal and conscious agents do exist, separate from impersonal and unconscious objects, why may not God exist as a proper, personal, and conscious being, separate from and ruling over the kingdoms of nature? Is man a personal and conscious being, while God has a mixed identity—conscious and unconscious at the same time! To argue that because one man is white and another is black, therefore George Washington could be neither a white man nor a black man, would be the exact counterpart of the author's reasoning when he utters the nonsense, that because personal agents and impersonal objects both exist, therefore God is neither, or that He is both.

To doubt of the personality of God, and His conscious separateness from matter, is to plunge the human reason back into the blindness of an atheistic philosophy. The wisdom of the ancients, of which Plato is the highest exponent, after ages of discussion, reached the conclusion that plan was before organization, a designer before a construction. And if there be such a thing as an intuition, which we ought to admit, notwithstanding the word is sadly abused by the transcendentalists, this is one: the designer is before and apart from the design. Man is conscious of designing, and then of moulding unconscious matter into the forms of the mental archetype. We are so made, that it is not possible for any one to perceive clearly the marks of design in any object, without the accompanying conviction that plan was before the construction. Whether we call this conviction, intuition, experience, or a logical deduction, the result is still the same: common reason teaches every man, what philosophy sanctions as the result of her most profound inquiries, that a designing cause is before and apart from a designed effect. Reason affirms design in nature. To write skeptically, therefore, concerning the conscious personality of God, as these writers do, is a sin against reason and philosophy, as well as against common sense and religion.

But there are scientific facts, ascertained beyond question, which should dispel the vague notions of those who speak of God as the "materiality of matter," and as being "inseparable from nature." An extract from "God Revealed in the Process of Creation, and by the Manifestation of Christ," will, I think, show that the idea of a God who is neither conscious nor unconscious, in the common acceptation of language, is no more in consonance with the facts of science than it is with the deductions of right reason.

The "Natural Development" theory, which argues that nature has been advanced from lower to higher species, by some law or power which is inseparable from the material universe, and which has developed itself from inanimate matter, up through an ascending series from the lowest to the highest genera of things, issues itself in an utter absurdity. "God is inseparable from nature," says the author of the "Vestiges." To this agree Compte, and probably such philosophers as Nott, Gliddon, and multitudes of others, like Mr. Emerson, who know little or nothing of the scientific basis of the argument.

And now let us notice some legitimate results of this theory, supposing it to be true. The whole subject is discussed at length in the volume referred to. The following is a passage from chapter viii:

"When it is said 'God can not be separated from nature,' while at the same time He is affirmed to be the 'author and sustainer of nature,' the import must be, according to this theory, that God has exercised no personal act of creation or control, since gravitation first affected the material which formed our system; or, if the theory be confined to the earth, then no creative act has been put forth by the Maker since the first organic cell was formed, and that was not formed by a divine author, but by law. God is declared to be 'Nature.' It is said that He is inseparable from nature, and that nature is the manifestation of God. Hence, as a logical necessity, natural phenomena, organic and inorganic, manifest all the God that belongs to this theory.

"If, then, God be inseparable from material nature now, He has been inseparable from nature in all the geologic periods of past progress. Then what follows? Why this: Reason is a product of material development; hence, before the existence of organic forms, there was no reason in existence; none, at least, in any wise connected with our planet. Intelligence was developed from lower susceptibilities up to higher instincts, and thence up to the human mind. Then, as a necessary sequent of this doctrine, it follows, that at early periods of creative progress, intelligence did not exist, and if God can not be separated from nature, then before nature produced intelligence, there was no intelligent God. During the Saurian Age, the lizard mind was the highest in existence; and if there be nothing above and separate from nature, then the fish-lizard-god was, in the secondary geological series the supreme being; or at least the supremest being that acted in connection with the earth.

But, is it said that not only the laws and beings of our earth, but the laws and beings of our whole system, or of the universe, are included in the idea of 'progressive development,' and that with this enlarged conception, God can not be separated from nature? Now, admitting the idea to be expanded, then, if God can not be separated from nature, He is in different stages of development in the universe at the same time. He is in different stages of development at the same time in our solar system, as the earth is in a different stage of progress from the moon; thus, in either view, the idea is an absurdity.

The legitimate ultimatum of any theory that recognizes the law of progressive development in creation as a power developing new and higher species out of lower ones, and which affirms at the same time that 'God is nature' and 'inseparable from nature,' thus placing divine interposition out of the question, the ultimatum of such a theory is, that as law has produced new species progressively from the mollusk to the man, so the future will be as the past; the latter product rising above previous ones, until the laws of nature will create a God, instead of God creating nature.

"What a rest to the soul is the rational, philosophical, and scriptural view, compared with such atheistic monstrosities. A true science predicates matter and its properties in the beginning; force developed and laws instituted by the dispositions of matter; organic life and progress from lower to higher forms; that progress in nature effected by the instrumentality of natural forces and laws; the method of advance by the destruction of lower and the introduction of higher species;—the whole produced, advanced, and controlled by laws, and in accordance with a plan which bears the impress of a Supreme Creator and Governor of the universe."

There are likewise, moral considerations connecting themselves with this subject which add to the difficulties of skepticism, while they accumulate proofs of the personal existence of the Divine Being.

Reason can account for things as they are, only upon one of three theories.

1. Chance, or the undetermined succession of events, in which nothing is settled, but every thing happens fortuitously and without design.

2. An omnipotent fate or law, sometimes called necessity, or the necessity of things, which causes and determines each event to exist invariably as it does; and which must thus cause all events in matter and mind forever.

3. A supreme intelligent Creator and Lawgiver, who governs the universe by laws adapted to the nature of things.

The first of these theories needs no discussion. The second theory has been proposed by skeptical inquirers ever since the birth of philosophy. It is still held in some form by atheists, by materialists, by those who believe in a law-soul of the world; and more recently by some who seem to believe that the machine of the universe being started, its own impulse produces all phenomena and all results which are exhibited in the worlds of matter and of mind.

Supposing this theory to be true, what do we learn concerning the moral character of God, and the condition and prospects of man?

He who doubts the existence of a personal God, is placed by that doubt in a peculiar position before his own consciousness:—he is a creature without a Creator, a child without a father, and an effect without a cause. But leaving laconics which need explanation, it will not be denied that man is a mortal and dependent being. He did not cause his own existence, and he is liable at any moment to suffer detriment in mind and body by laws or circumstances over which he has no control. If there be no personal God who administers a moral government which differs from the allotments of nature, then man is plainly the victim of a power that is malignant in its nature. Call that power what you please, the "substantiality of matter," as Mr. Parker would say; or the impersonal nature of things, as Mirabaud and Compte would assert. A personal God separate from nature being ignored, then the nature of things is a power, man is subject to that power, and that power is evil *per se*, and evil in development. If this blind power be called God, it can be described by adding a single adjective to the definition of materialists. "God, neither personal nor impersonal, conscious nor unconscious"—but malignant.

In order to see the ground of this affirmation, notice in connection with it, the phenomena of conscience. If all things occur by a force of nature, or by any impersonal force operating through nature, a man should suffer no more for an evil act than a good one. If a parent were to force, or even influence his child to do a certain action, and then punish him for doing it, such a father would be a monster. It has been replied to this, that a man suffers compunction of conscience because he believes an act to be wrong, and thus believing, it is righteousness, in the nature of things, which causes him to suffer for it. But evidently this reply only removes the difficulty one step further back. According to this system, a man's faith, good or bad, is produced as much by a force of nature and circumstance as his actions; hence, the compunction of conscience is still the result of a necessitated antecedent. Nature, therefore, which attaches remorse to an act which she herself produces, either immediately or by a chain of causes, is just as malignant as a parent would be if he influenced his son to do a wrong action and then punished him for doing it. If man be a voluntary moral agent, and sin a moral evil, the office of conscience in admonishing of sin and denouncing the sinner, is an evidence of the mercy and justice of God. But if man be not a personal agent, if God be not a personal sovereign, the conscience is not only a mystery, but a malignity.

It is, moreover, a law of man's moral nature that the more he loves evil, and the more frequently he sins, the less he suffers from the inflictions of conscience. If, then, there be beyond this law of nature no God who is the moral governor and judge of men, then this nature of things is evidently malignant; because many men grow more selfish and wicked till they die, and the more evil they become, the less remorse they feel for sin. Nature thus makes sin the way of life. Despots succeed in crushing out light and liberty by banishing the master-spirits of the age, and shedding rivers of human blood, as those heartless adventurers the Bonapartes, and I had almost written, some of their despicable American biographers. And yet, thousands of widows and orphans suffer thousands of times more in consequence of their evil acts than they do themselves. Who dare say that if this be the work of nature beyond which there is no God, that nature is not malignant? In charity we accept some of Mr. Parker's best definitions as his prevailing idea of God; but when he becomes a materialist with Mirabaud, or a pantheist, or law-soulist with Chambers and Compte, then, instead of writing down his impersonal God as "knowledge, love, power," he should write power, law, malignity.

But furthermore, and finally, and conclusively, unless the Maker has incorporated a falsehood into the human soul, man is a free, responsible agent, and God is a personal moral governor. Man is so constituted, that he can not feel guilty for wrong, unless he is conscious that he was voluntary in the wrong act. If, therefore, he is not the responsible cause of his own moral action, God has placed a lying witness in his soul.

But look again at the irrefragible testimony which the human consciousness gives of the responsibility of man and the personality of God. Man is actually so constituted, as a moral being, that obedience and gratitude can be exercised only toward a personal being, a being who personally and voluntarily does us good. Can man be grateful to the bread that satisfies his hunger? Can he love and obey something that is neither personal nor impersonal in any comprehensible sense? The thought is preposterous! Unless the moral nature of man be a lie, produced by malignity, there is a personal conscious God, to obey and love whom is the life and adaptation of the human soul.

Is it not ridiculous, as well as preposterous, to think of the author of this book expatiating upon the nature of God, with the exhortation to love and obedience which must follow. He says, my hearers—"God is the ground of nature—He is what is permanent in the passing, what is real in the apparent." "God is the materiality of matter," so "He is the spirituality of spirit." But "He is neither personal nor conscious, like Peter and Joseph, nor impersonal and unconscious like the moss or the ether." "The greatest religious souls can say with an old heathen, 'Since God can not be fully declared by any one name, though compounded of never so many; therefore He is rather to be called by every name, He being both one and all things.'" The preacher then adds an exhortation, thus: "As I have always told you, my friends, love and obedience to God is the duty and happiness of man. You have heard my description of 'the dear God.' I enjoin upon you to love and obey The Materiality of Matter, the All Things, the Spirituality of Spirit, the neither personal nor impersonal, conscious nor unconscious God. Yea, my hearers, I say unto you obey it! It is immanent in all things—in the blush of the rose and in the bite of the dog—in the breath of the breeze and in the howl of the maniac. Remember, too, our party 'calls religion nature,' believes 'the divine incarnation is in all mankind,' 'asks no forgiveness for sin,' therefore we will imitate the divine incarnation, and if we sin we will ask no forgiveness. Amen and amen."

Now, if this be preposterous, it is so because it is an application of Unitarian Rationalism in the light of common sense. If any one says that passages are so clustered together as to make them seem preposterous, we deny the impeachment. Other results may be obtained by inferences from other passages, but the above is a fair and unavoidable result from one class of passages written in this volume.

And besides, there are single passages which are as preposterous in themselves as these are put together, and not only in this volume, but they are found in nearly all this class of writers. In one of his Ten Sermons, for instance, the author says of a fly, "Lo! here I am an individual and conscious thing, sucking the bosom of the world." This is certainly hyperbole run mad; and is just about as ridiculous as it would be to say of the eminent Mr. Emerson; "Lo! there he is, an individual and conscious philosophist, sucking transcendentalism from the great toe of the—man in the moon."

Such nonsense produced by men of ability,

capable of writing eloquently, sensibly, and consistently, is only another evidence that without faith, the mind is like a ship without ballast, driven by contrary winds. Let us turn away from such hallucinations—hallucinations that mingle the evil and the incongruous with the good, and rejoice together in the evidence, that above the laws of nature, there presides a supreme, personal God, the parent, and the president of the universe.

There are moral evidences derived from the nature of man, besides those to which we have alluded, that affirm the divine personality; evidences in which all good and thoughtful men will rejoice together, although the doubts and difficulties interposed by skeptics were a thousand fold greater than they are. God exists as a personal being with moral attributes: He is just,

1. Because He has connected the monitions and reproofs of conscience, with actions known to be wrong.

2. Because if conscience be not heeded, it leaves the transgressor to grow hardened in evil; evil which in itself is incipient penalty, and which being voluntarily persisted in, becomes confirmed in the character of the transgressor.

3. Because motives to good, if obeyed become more influential; if disobeyed, less so.

4. Because the moral constitution is so formed that the more sinful men become, the more blind they become, both to the evil and the desert of sin.

5. Because evil is not only linked with sin and penalty here, but while it brings present evil, it also forms an evil character in the soul, which secures future evil.

Finally—God is good—

Because love is happiness and life, and He has made the soul so that its best good consists in a life of love to God and to men. And as love begets love, God becomes immanently personal in Christ, in whose sacrifice He reveals divine love, and thus by faith, love is begotten, and the law of love is fulfilled in all "who walk not after the flesh, but after the Spirit.

Is not such evidence, and the known practical results of the Christian faith, a satisfaction to the reason and a joy to the heart, while the brilliant vagaries of skeptical thinkers are empty and evil continually?

CHAPTER VII.

THE TRI-UNITY OF THE DIVINE MIND.

I now propose to offer some reasons affirmatory of the orthodox faith, with the design more especially to illustrate and defend some of the doctrines which are controverted or rejected by the skeptics of our times.

In what I shall say I do not propose to give a scriptural exposition of these doctrines, nor to present them in the form of a dogmatic statement; nor do I propose to illustrate or confirm the symbols of any particular denomination.

Illustrations are seldom perfectly accurate; and reasons which should be limited to certain aspects of a question, may be missapplied to cover the whole subject. My design, therefore, will not be to prove the systematic form of the doctrines of which I shall speak; but to show that the evangelical interpretation of the Scriptures, as generally expressed in the formularies of the churches, has illustrative and analogical reasoning on its side. I desire to show that reason is with the evangelical system, and not against it; and that many aspects of vital Christian doctrine, as expressed in the New Testament may be sustained by accurate deduction, and illustrated by the most profound analogies.

Let us look first at the doctrine of the Trinity. This doctrine is contained in the general expression that there is one God, one name, Jehovah, who is manifested in the Scriptures as subsisting in three divine persons, the Father, the Son, the Holy Ghost.

It is agreed that the word person is used in dogmatic theology, not because its common import conveys a perfect sense of the doctrine as revealed in the New Testament; but because it conveys a sense, which, being defined by the phrases of the Scriptures, gives an accurate idea. It is, moreover, the most proper, we may say the only proper word, because the sacred writers all use the pronouns which the laws of language require should be used in a personal sense in substitution for Father, Son, and Spirit. No other word in any language will generalize the expressions of the sacred writers. They apply the personal pronouns to Father, Son, and Holy Spirit, while yet they give to each of these the attributes of the one name—Jehovah. It is easy for men to declaim against the doctrine of the Trinity, but so long as they can not deny this usage of the inspired writers, there is a Scriptural basis for the orthodox interpretation.

We affirm, then, that there is in the divine nature a basis for the tri-personal manifestation of God, and that it is only by the manifestation of God in three persons that the divine nature can be efficaciously known.*

*The Andover exposition of Schleiermacher, in the notes of Professor Stuart, affirms a basis in the divine mind for the triune manifestation of God to men; and affirms, likewise, the adaptations of this divine manifestation to the wants of humanity. "Tri-unity, according to my humble apprehension, consists in something that belongs to the *Monos* itself, and which laid the foundations for the manifestations of Father, and Son, and Spirit." "Who can refuse to acknowledge that either some modification or some property of the divine nature in respect to substance or attribute general enough, certainly, led to the manifestation of the Godhead in what we call a personal manner?"

Dr. Bushnell, of Hartford, who gives Schleiermacherism blinded by an imperfect conception, doubts this, as he does the proper humanity of Christ. In our humble opinion, Andover is right in its conception of the basis of the divine manifestation and of the person of the Redeemer.

It has been true in times past, that the fear of the power which graceless dogmatics have exercised to create odium against reason, has prevented many who love the truth from conceding the

It is well known that in the age of Plato, when reason reached her culminating point among the ancients, the idea of the tri-unity of God was strikingly approximated. Now, while this fact does not prove that the depths of the divine can be fathomed by the finite human, we think it does prove that the most profound indications of the light of nature, point in the direction of orthodox Christian doctrine.*

The Philonic exposition is grounded in the phraseology of the Old Testament—the Platonic in the constitution of the human mind. Both of these bear the impress of the Maker's mind,

value of the elder developments of the human reason on this and kindred subjects, that of Plato and Philo, for instance ; but so long as it is true that the Talmudic and Alexandrine exposition of the *Logos* gives the *usus loquendi* of apostolic times, the man departs from the correct laws of interpretation who refuses to acknowledge the fact.

* The seeds of the philosophy of Philo are found in the Old Testament, while his system, if he really has one, is developed in Platonic phraseology. Philo, in some passages, undoubtedly attributes personality to the logos ; and it must be conceded that the Apostle John coincides in conception more nearly with Philo than he does with some symbolic expressions of later times, even of our times.

We might speak, too, of some of the most profound thinkers among the Unitarians, who have intimated in impressive circumstances, and in imposing positions, a desire to be understood as approximating the Trinitarian views of the Godhead.—*See Channing and Bancroft's Addresses.*

and hence analogies derived from these sources are founded in truth. We do not affirm that they are always rightly applied.

"The physical universe," it is said, "as well as the moral, bears upon its nature the impress of the Creator." Certainly it does, and those who are disposed to pantheistic notions—who tell their hearers that "nature is religion," and who find "God immanent in all things"—will, of course, favor analogies from the nature of material things to the nature of God. But when they say, that "a simple monad lies at the origin of all natural phenomena," the illustration is clearly at fault. If the atomic philosophy be true, there is an infinity of atoms, and likewise a diversity in their qualities.

The elementary principles of matter may be separated the one from the other, by chemical processes, and each of these, perhaps, has a molecular constitution; but the actual economic entities of the physical world are mostly triunities. The elements of the phenomenal world were not created to exist in separate unities, but to combine in the forms in which matter is manifested to man. The elementary principles prove by their affinities that they abhor absolute unity.

Some two elements, with electricity, the everywhere-present spirit of matter, combine to form the character of material things, as manifested to the human sense. The earth, air, water, are trinities, or rather tri-unities. They have qualities as unities and qualities as tri-unities. The elements of things were not designed to exist alone. They seek tri-unity in one spirit by their inherent affinities. And in tri-unity alone is nature practically adapted to humanity. Physical nature is mostly manifested by tri-unity.

The evangelical view of the Godhead does not need that we should plead this analogy in its support; but the fact that matter is manifested, in many instances, by a tri-unity, and that the nature of elementary things is such that they seek union in a trinity, and that it is only in this form that they have, for the most part, a practical value and relation to other things—this, we affirm, proves this much, viz., the analogies of the physical world are opposed to those who argue from nature, for absolute unity in the manifestation or in the nature of God. The awful solitude of one individual, elementary essence is a thought against which the heart and reason reluctate.

Suppose we look into the intellectual world, and inquire whether there are not analogies here that connect themselves with this subject?

Reason is an absolute unity. Love is an absolute unity. Will is an absolute unity. These are the same in themselves, and the same in all moral beings. They are separable from each other, and yet united in one consciousness. Human reason, love, and will, are finite, and they may be perverted in finite beings, but they are the same in their nature whether they inhere in a finite, or in an infinite being.

The oldest Scripture declares that man was created in the moral image of God. To infer, therefore, the moral nature of the Maker from the moral nature of man, is not only warranted by the fact that reason, will, and love must be the same in kind in all beings, but it is warranted likewise by the statements of revelation. Now, while we do not find the human nature manifesting itself tri-personally, yet we do find humanity manifested in a tripartite form. And thus reason has a basis in the finite for accepting what is revealed concerning the infinite.

Again: Man is one in nature. He is conscious of oneness in himself, while yet his nature is such that it can be made known or revealed to others only by a tri-fold manifestation. To love is a different thing from to know; and to know differs both from to will and to love; yet it is the one man that thinks, wills, and loves. And not only this, but while these powers of the human mind are diverse from each other, yet the whole man acts in each of them, the whole man thinks, wills, or loves.

We may know a man by his intellectual manifestation, while we know little or nothing of his affections and will—nothing of his moral character. This is experienced sometimes when we read an unknown author. We only know a man's nature truly, when he has revealed himself to us in his threefold manifestation of intellect, sensibility, and will.

This analogy is but introductory. It does not, in my opinion, give a correct idea of the Trinity. A better analogy than this can be derived from the economy of moral natures. The logos of of the mind, the mental exercises or ideas, is not the same as the conscious I in the soul of man. Thought is born of man's conscious nature, as the light is born of the sun. But in moral beings there is something in the nature that stands back of thought, and judges of its character and fitness. I see my thoughts and judge of them.* The I that sees and judges of the product of the mind is as separate from the thought, in one sense, as the subject is from the object. In their relation to each other, the one is begotten of the substance of the other; yet they are in a true sense one; one is the manifestation of the other; one is the vital image or living exhibition of the other. The unknown one in the human or in the divine nature can be made known only by this manifestation; and yet the true character of this logos, or son of the mind, is known only to the unknown one. This philosophy Jesus teaches as true of Himself in his relation to the Father. "No man knoweth the Son but the Father; and no man knoweth the Father but the Son, and he to whomsoever the Son will reveal him."

Again, while the logos, or conceived ideas, is neither the affections nor the will, yet will and affection are manifested through and by the in-

* This thought undoubtedly possessed the devout Baxter when he advised his friends "to be none of those who shall charge with heresy all who say the three persons in the Godhead are—God understanding himself, God understood by himself, and God loving himself."

telligence. The logos is the out-birth of the moral nature, and it is through the logos that the tenderness of the affection and the determination of the will are made known to others. The logos is an out-birth. Will and love are a procession of the moral nature through the logos. They are seen in the intelligence, and manifested by it. *

The Scriptural statement then may be affirmed as profoundly accordant with the analogies of nature. "In the beginning was the Word, and the Word was with God, and the Word was God." Then there is the Word conceived, and the Word revealed or manifested.†

* We purposely, for the most part, avoid the imperfect definitions of mental philosophy, and use such words as we hope may be plain to common readers. Such as will refer each reader to his own consciousness.

† Matthew Henry, the best read in the Bible of all the commentators, has clearly conceived and distinctly stated the inspired conception in the first of John. We give the passage in full, for the benefit of any who seldom refer to this most biblical of all the commentators.

"The Chaldee paraphrase very frequently calls the Messia the Word of Jehovah, and speaks of many things in the Old Testament said to be done by the Lord, as done by the Word of the Lord. Even the vulgar Jews were taught that the Word of God was the same with God. The evangelist, in the close of his discourse, *John* 1: 18, plainly tells us why he calls Christ the Word of God, because he is the only-begotten Son which is in the bosom of the Father, and has declared him. Word is two-fold, word conceived and word uttered.

Some passages from the ancients, held at the time when the primitive church was exercising the power which converted the world, will give the mode of thinking among the best men of that age. The following beautiful passage is a true translation from the Exhortation of Clement of Alexandria to the Greeks: "The divine Logos—the Christ—was the cause of our being, and our well-being also, for he was in God; and now this Logos himself appears to men; the

(1.) There is the word conceived: that is thought, which is the only immediate product of the soul, all the operations of which are performed by thought, and it is one with the soul. Thus the second person in the Trinity is fitly called the Word; for he is the first-begotten of the Father; that eternal wisdom which the Lord possessed, as the soul doth its thought in the beginning of his way, *Prov.* viii. 22. There is nothing we are more sure of than that we think, yet nothing we are more in the dark about than how we think; who can declare the generation of thought in the soul? Surely then the generations and births of the eternal mind may well be allowed to be great mysteries of godliness, which we can not fathom, while yet we adore the depth.

(2.) There is the word uttered, and that is speech. Thus Christ is the Word, for by him God has in these last days spoken to us, *Heb.* i. 2, and has directed us to hear him, *Matt.* xvii. 5. He has made known God's mind to us, as a man's word or speech makes known his thoughts, as far as he pleases, and no farther. Christ is called that wonderful speaker, *Dan.* viii. 23, the speaker of things hidden and strange. He is the Word speaking from God to us, and to God for us. John Baptist was the voice; but Christ the Word; being the Word, he is the Truth, the Amen, the faithful Witness of the mind of God."

only being that ever partook of both natures, as well that of God as of man; to be the cause of all good to us. From him we learn to live virtuously; by him we are conducted in the way of eternal life; as saith the divine apostle of the Lord, 'The love of God the Saviour was manifested to all men, instructing us in order that we, having abjured all impiety and worldly desires, might live soberly and piously in this world, expecting in blessed hope the manifestation of the glory of our great God and Saviour Jesus Christ.'"

Tertullian says: "The Greeks term that Logos which we translate Word, and thus our people, i. e. the Christians, for brevity sake, say, 'In the beginning the Word was with God,' though it would be more proper to say reason, since God was not speaking from the beginning, although rational. * * * Considering, therefore, and disposing by his reason, he effected his will by his Word, which thou mayest easily understand by what passes in thyself. * * * when thou conferrest silently with thine own reason."—*Tertul. adv. Praxeam*, c. v.

Says Justin, *Ap. ii.*: "It is not allowable, therefore, to think otherwise of the Spirit and the Power which is in God, than that it is the Logos, which also is the first-born of God."

"That distinction in the nature of God which would lead to His development as Father, Son, and Holy Spirit, and which fitted him for this, existed from all eternity, and was an inseparable part of His nature; but Father, Son, and Holy Ghost, in the full sense of the ecomomy of the gospel, He actually was not, until the incarnation of the Logos, and the outpouring of the Spirit had been actually completed."—*M. Stuart.*

The origin of the conceived Word is as old as the divine mind. He was in the beginning with God, the eternally-begotten Son of the Father. But the revealed or manifested Word is no older in His relations to men, than the time when the character of the divine mind was manifested to men by its Logos. "No man hath seen God at any time; the only-begotten Son, which is in the bosom of the Father, He hath declared him."

Man can embody his Logos impersonally in written language, and send it thus embodied to all nations who understand the written character. Why then might not the "Word of God become flesh?" Why might not the Son of God thus become personally incarnate, so that the affections and will of the Father might be expressed in him and through him, not impersonally but personally, in life and power? The Scriptures affirm, what a true reason approves, that the Word of God did become flesh, and that Christ is the "out-shining of the Father's glory, and the express image of His person." "He that hath seen Christ hath seen the Father." The embodiment of man's Logos in language is only vital with intelligence. The embodiment of the divine Logos in the flesh, is the revealment of the "fullness of the Godhead bodily"—the logos in a nature in which can be manifested not only the intelligence but the affection and will of God.

Let us advance one step further, and look at this thought in another aspect. Jesus said to His disciples, "It is expedient for you that I go away, for if I go not away, the Holy Spirit, or Comforter, will not come unto you; and if I go away I will send Him unto you; but when He is come, He will not speak of Himself, but He will take of the things that belong to me, and show them unto you."

Thus the Spirit is represented not as a revealer

of new truth, but as a personal procession from the Father through the Son into the hearts of believers. He takes the facts furnished by the Logos, and, by a revealment of life and love, gives efficacy, as divine power and love alone can do, to the truth as it is in Jesus. The Son, spiritually concieved, is eternally begotten of the Father, the same in nature with him, and the only revealer of the Father. The Holy Spirit comes to us in power and love, baptized in the humanities of Christ, being revealed in and through the Son. Christ furnishes the material for redemption—the facts which reveal the divine nature. The Holy Spirit applies them in the soul. Hence, Christ and the Holy Spirit dwelling in believers, are interchangeable terms in the New Testament. The Father and the Son are likewise interchangeable. "I am in the Father and the Father in me." So "the grace of our Lord Jesus Christ, and the love of God the Father, and the communion of the Holy Ghost," are with those who believe. Such undoubtedly, is the apostolic conception.

Let us look again into the human consciousness, and listen again to the voice of reason, while we consider revealed truth in another aspect. Human nature, as constituted by its Maker, would certainly be fitted to appreciate the divine character. The moral relations between God and man, the one being a sovereign, the other a subject, require this; and the fitness of things observable throughout the creation, assure us that there would be fitness between revelation and human comprehension. An argument, therefore, for the Trinity may be found in its adaptations to the mental constitution and moral necessities of man. Let us inquire then for the value of the doctrine of Father, Son, and Spirit as adapted to meet the finite apprehension of men, and to aid them in approximating a true knowledge of the character of God.

The mind of man has a logical conformation. It is made to ratiocinate—to develop processes of synthesis, analysis, and generalization. In studying the nature of any thing, we combine its manifestations, or phenomena, and thus gain a knowledge of its true character. This being the character of the mind, it is adapted by its constitution to attain ultimate knowledge of God through the revealed doctrine of the Trinity, in the same way by which it attains knowledge of other things, that is, by the exercise of its rational powers. If the knowledge of God's character, as well as his being, were by intuition, as superficial thinkers teach, man would not know the character of God as a reasoning being, but as an unreasoning animal.

The character of God is adapted to regenerate human nature, and adapted to regenerated nature; hence man's rational nature is profoundly adapted to the doctrine of the Trinity. The mind of man can not apprehend the divine character, nor the relations of God to his creatures, by a single conception. Even the character and relations of an earthly ruler can not be compassed by one grasp of the mind. Victoria is not only Regina, but she is Defender of the Faith and Patroness of the great charities of her queendom. We speak of Victoria because she is a rare instance of a virtuous sovereign, while she combines in her person regal, spiritual, and benevolent prerogative. In order to form a true idea of the character of this sovereign, and of her relations to her realm, we must form the distinct conception of three regal offices, and of the queen acting personally in each of these, and then combine these several conceptions in one character.* By this illustration we do not, of course, mean to be understood that the Christhood is only God acting officially; while this is true, yet it is, as we have shown, also true that Christ is Logos, the revealer of the Godhead bodily and personally. The statement is presented to prove a fact which is verified in the experience of every man: a fact, the consideration of which ought to influence the mind of skeptics to a right conclusion, that the mind of man is so constituted, that the triune manifestation of God is adapted to enable him as a rational being to comprehend God; and that by this manifestation he can approximate the absolute truth, far beyond any attainment he could make by his own unaided conception.

That man can have no just idea of God, who endeavors to compass the divine mind in a single thought. The bare idea of power and Godhead, transfers the mind back from the third to the first dispensation, when the Almighty was known

* It would, perhaps, be more proper to say that person is an intuition or coetaneous conception always present in the mind, when we conceive of a moral being; and the three offices attach them selves by a mental necessity to the one name of Victoria; and then the character of Victoria must be derived from her action in them all.

as God of Creation only; as Jehovah, He was more perfectly revealed to Moses, in the second dispensation; as God in Christ, He is most perfectly revealed in the New Testament. After we have apprehended God as the Father Almighty, and conceived of him as truth and love in Christ, and as an every-where-present life and power in the Spirit; after the soul has appreciated and appropriated, by faith, all that there is in Father, Son, and Holy Ghost, then only it has arisen to the best knowledge that a finite mind can gain of the character of the true God. Hence it is written, "Go teach all nations, baptizing them into the one name but three persons, the Father, the Son, the Holy Ghost, and lo! I am with you always, even to the end of the dispensation."

The Christian alone, who has faith in God, as revealed in the New Testament, obtains an adequate, and vitalizing knowledge of the divine character. The God of one intuition or conception is an abstract nullity, devoid of all moral power over human character and human life. The God of one intuition, with the superadded characteristics which man's folly or his philosophy always frames when he is devoid of faith in revelation, is more or less an erroneous and corrupting conception. Christianity alone enlightens the natural mind, guides the reason, and matures the conception of the divine character. Hence the idea of God, as conceived by liberal Christians who reject revealed religion, is incongruous and foolish. The Christian alone rises by faith and reason to a knowledge of the living and true God, clothed in his attributes of power, light, and love.

Shall we not, then, turn away from the hallucinations of the skeptics, and the conceited rationalisms of transcendentalists, and seek in the Scriptures the knowledge of God, "whom to know aright, as Father, Son, and Spirit, is life eternal."

CHAPTER VIII.

HUMAN DEPRAVITY.

The doctrine of human depravity is rejected contemptuously by many so-called liberal Christians in our day; and with these there are many good and thoughtful men who misapprehend its import, and hence doubt of its truth. This latter class is led into doubt upon this subject about as much by the overstrained definition of some orthodox preachers, as they are by the same fault on the part of those who oppose Christianity as a system of revealed religion.

There is a basis in human reason and experience, as well as in revelation, for this doctrine; and neither the mis-statements of the friends of Christianity, nor the mal-statements of its enemies, can invalidate the facts and reasons upon which the doctrine rests.

The statement that men are by nature averse

to all good, and as evil as it is possible for them to be, is not true to the common sense of men, nor in the common use of language. Such expressions may be explained into accordance with the Scriptures, but it is far better to avoid the extreme expression to which every denomination, from the very nature of selfishness, is prone to carry its own distinguishing tenets, and present the Christian doctrines in such phraseology as falls clearly within the import of the facts and texts upon which they are grounded.

While, therefore, there may be some apology for misapprehension on this subject, there can be no good apology for such statements as that of the writer in the book before me, viz., "The popular religion is hostile to man; tells us he is an outcast; not a child of God, but a spurious issue of the devil."

The most trustworthy writers on this subject always state the question in its connections, and with the limitations which experience and the Bible require. Dr. Chalmers, in speaking of those who are unregenerated, says: "The principle upon which you may have acted may be respectable and honorable and amiable. We are not disputing all this. We are only saying that it is not the love of God. And should we hear any one of you assert that I have nothing to reproach myself with, and that I give every body their own, and that I possess a fair character in society, and have done nothing to forfeit it; and that I have my share of generosity and honor, of tenderness and civility: our only reply is, that this may be very true; you may have a very large share of these and of other estimable principles, but along with the possession of these many things, you may lack one thing, and that one thing may be the love of God. An enlightened discerner of the heart may look into you and say with our Savior, 'I know you that ye have not the love of God in you.'"

We will give another extract from a writer generally accepted among evangelical Christians —one of the most clear-minded and pure-hearted men of his age. These extracts are given at length, in order that we may consider this subject unbiased by the fear that the views which we shall present do not apply to the subject as generally received by enlightened Christians.

We do not, as we have already said, present our views as an exposition of the symbols of any one denomination; some of the creeds were wrought out by good men in a darker age than the present. We write to show that the doctrine of human depravity, as revealed in the Scriptures and expounded by men of spiritual apprehension, accords with reason and with human experience.

Dr. Dwight says: "The human character is not depraved to the full extent of the human powers. It has been said, neither unfrequently nor by men void of understanding, that man is as depraved a being as his faculties will permit him to be; but this has been said without consideration and without truth. Neither Scripture nor experience warrant the assertion. 'Wicked men and deceivers,' it is declared, 'wax worse and worse, deceiving and being deceived.' During the first half of human life this may, perhaps, be explained by the growth of the faculties, but during a considerable period preceding its termination it can not thus be explained, for the faculties decay while the depravity still increases." "The young man who came to Christ to know what good thing he should do to inherit eternal life, was certainly less depraved than his talents would have permitted him to be.

"Like him, we see daily many men who

neither are nor profess to be Christians, and who, instead of being wicked to a degree commensurate with their faculties, go through life in the exercise of dispositions so sincere, just, and amiable, and in the performance of actions so upright and beneficent, as to secure a high degree of respect and affection from ourselves, and from all with whom they are connected. It certainly can not be said that such men are as sinful as many others possessed of powers far inferior, much less that they are as sinful as they can be. Those who make the assertion against which I am contending, will find themselves, if they will examine, rarely believing that their wives and children, though not Christians, are fiends."

Again, Dr. Dwight says; "Some of the natural human characteristics are amiable. Such are natural affection; the simplicity and sweetness of disposition in children, often found also in persons of adult years; compassion, generosity, modesty, and what is sometimes called natural conscientiousness, that is, a fixed and strong sense of the importance of doing that which is right. These characteristics appear to have adorned the young man whom I have already mentioned.

We know that they are amiable, because we are informed that 'Jesus, beholding him, loved him.' In the same manner we, and all others who are not abandoned, love them always and irresistibly, whenever they are presented to our view. They all, also, are required, and exist in every Christian, enhancing his holiness and rendering him a better man. Without them it is not easy to perceive how the Christian character could exist. Accordingly, Paul exhibits those who are destitute of these attributes as being literally profligate."

If, then, the doctrine of human depravity, as expounded by the accepted teachers of the orthodox faith, does not affirm that man's faculties are wholly depraved; if it be a manifest, and indubitable fact that men may possess by nature many excellent and amiable qualities for which we ought to love them; what then is the scriptural, rational, and experimental import of the doctrine of human depravity, and in what sense are all men depraved?

It is affirmed in the Scriptures, and all men adopt the principle as a tenet of absolute religion, that man shall love God with all his heart, and his neighbor as himself. Of the obligation of this requirement there can be no doubt. God is the supreme being, and the best being, and, therefore, of right demands supreme love. The interests of other men are as valuable to them as our interests are to us; hence they should be regarded equally with our own. This is the moral law of the universe. To this all agree. Now, the question is not whether some men have not by nature many good qualities, nor whether any man is as bad as he could be? But the question is, whether men do by nature love and obey God? whether they are by nature conformed or unconformed to the moral law of God?

The question, when fairly stated, is a very plain one; and the man who doubts of human depravity in the light of a true statement, can have but little apprehension either of God's character or of his own. If men loved and obeyed the true God by nature, they would have to make an effort not to love and obey him. Every body knows that the reverse of this is true, and that the effort is on the other side of the question. But while argument may not make a palpable experience more plain to Christians, it may promote right conviction with those who are not. Let us, then, look first at the testimony of universal consciousness.

I need not recite those passages from the ancient classics with which all scholars are familiar. Epictetus, speaking of the consciousness of every natural mind in which the moral sense is not obliterated, says, almost in the words of Paul, or rather Paul says, almost in his words, "He that sins does not what he would, but what he would not, that he does." In accordance with this speak all the worthy ancients who have given us their self-consciousness on moral subjects.

Take again the testimony of univeral history. It can not be doubted that humanity has always been found by the light of history and revelation in a corrupted moral state. We mean, distinctly, in a state entirely destitute of supreme love to God as a holy sovereign, and to men as brothers. That civilization made progress in some old nations—that intellectual light and a perception of moral truths were in some minds clear and strong, is granted; but the knowledge of God, the disposition to love men as brethren, and a prevalent regard for moral purity, is not the natural state of man. The fact is striking as it is indubitable, that the most enlightened nations, as they increase in years, invariably, without the aid of revelation, become more corrupt. And as they add years, they add evil to their national life. And even now, in lands professing to receive the religion of Christ, and among those who recognize the obligation to love God as the common Father, and all men as brethren—even in Christendom, notwithstanding an assent to right principles, war and lust, pride and self-seeking, are the rule, and obedience to the recognized moral law of love is the exception.

Leaving the universal law of love out of the question, which is the recognized standard of duty, and to which man would be conformed if he, by nature, knew and obeyed the true God; even setting this aside, it is true that men have in all ages been conscious of being unconformed to their own knowledge of duty. This is evidenced by the fact, that the human consciousness of sin in all time, until Christ's sacrifice, has been evinced by the sacrifice of victims, human and bestial, as expiatory or propitiatory offerings, to procure reconciliation with God.

This testimony of universal consciousness,

* See "Philosophy of Plan of Salvation," Chap. I.

universal history, and universal conduct, can not go for nothing. To make a light thing of the deepest and most solmenly-expressed convictions of human nature, is to be untrue to humanity as it is. The human consciousness cries out for reconciliation with God. The man who answers that it needs none, is as injurious to the soul as a physician would be to the body, who, in a dangerous malady, should give opiates, and let the disease take its course.

If the liberal writer of these "Discourses of Religion" believed his own affirmations, we see not how he could avoid admitting the total depravity of human nature? Indeed, it is true that he, in statement, apparently unconcious that almost his whole book is in contradiction to this, utters words affirming the depravity of humanity and the necessity of Christ's death. He says, "The history of society is summed up in a word—Cain killed Abel. That of real Christianity also in a word—Christ died for his brothers."

The direct inference from this liberal theology goes likewise to establish the opposite of what it teaches. If man has by intuition, or in some other way, a "true idea of God, which is the same in all men," then it follows as a fact corroborated by all history, that man must have propensities so totally depraved that they lead him to reject the true knowledge of the divine, and plunge into darkness and evil, notwithstanding the counter influence of the true idea of God. If this be not an evidence of depravity, we would humbly inquire what can be evidence in the case?

Perhaps the writer would refer us to the conception which he says man gets from nature, and then tell us that the conception obscures the intuition. Then two things follow—first, that all nature is depraved from which man gets the obscuring conception; and, second, that God has given man a true idea of himself, which is not strong enough to resist the depraving power of depraved nature.

But let us turn from the "variations" found in these Unitarian Radicals, and look at the appeal which may be made to each individual's consciousness in behalf of the doctrine of depravity.

Men will acknowledge that they do not live up to the amount of their knowledge; that they do not live up to their ability; that they do not live up to their conscience. Now, what is the reason of this? Who will answer? The brute lives up to the best instincts of his nature. The brute conforms by nature to the laws of his highest life and happiness. Why is not man thus conformed to the moral law of love? Why does he not by nature live a life like Christ? Let the reader frankly acknowledge that it is because the current of the human will runs in another direction. Hence it is the experience of every living man who seeks conformity to the will of God, that he must struggle against the inertia, and earthly and selfish propensions of his natural mind. And it is likewise, as we believe, an experience, that divine aid alone enables the soul to rise above the natural into the spiritual life.

We repeat, if there be any thing plain in the Scriptures, it is the struggle, or spiritual warfare, that is necessary to attain and maintain conformity to the will of God as manifested in Christ. If there be any thing true in Christian experience it is this same warfare—a warfare which reaches a conscious and joyful triumph only by faith in Christ, as a present divine Savior. If men by nature be not out of conformity with the law of God, then the whole tenor of the New Testament and all Christian experience are together false, because the one affirms what the other realizes.

But it is not possible to lead any man who has ever seriously endeavored to be like Christ, to doubt that by nature his will "is alienated from the life of God." Liberal Christians may lead men of no Christian purpose to doubt, but they can do no more. The man who permits his boat to float upon the current of Lake Superior, will move downward, without an effort, to the more rapid current of the Niagara river. He can not be conscious of any effort, because he makes none. It requires no effort to float with the current. But if a man will save himself from going over the falls, he must turn his boat against the stream, and his labors will grow light, and his hope and peace will increase, as he escapes the dangerous current, and sees on the farthermost verge of the lake the light-house near his home. So the Christian who has struggled against the natural current of the will, finds peace as he overcomes, and rejoices as the light grows brighter, which shines out from the "light-house in the sky."

The teachings of the Scriptures on this subject not only accord with experience, but they contain a profound philosophy, which will, by some future writer, be developed in a more satisfactory manner than it is at present. Allow me to present an allusion to this future philosophy.

Adam, the origin of our transmitted humanity, is said to have been a "living soul." Christ, the source of our spiritual and eternal life, is "a quickening Spirit." We inherit from Adam an earthly nature, whose appetites, motives, aspirations, are limited to the earth. This is, in the language of the New Testament, "the natural mind," "the old man," "the flesh." The first birth is natural, and gives to man only earthly and selfish instincts and aspirations. Man by nature may be an amiable and excellent earthly being, or he may be a morally deformed and despicable one; but still he is "of the earth earthy," and, as Jesus affirmed, "the love of God is not in him." He is "alive" to earthly and selfish motives and objects; but he is "dead unto God;" he does not feel and move in view of what God is, nor in view of what he has commanded. In his mind, his own will, not the will of God, is supreme; and he resists subjection to the will of God, as much as an animal *fere naturæ*, wild by nature, resists subjection to the will of man. The divine Teacher affirmed the foundational truth on this subject when he said, "That which is born of the flesh is flesh, that which is born of the Spirit is spirit."

Christ, the second Adam, is a "life-giving Spirit;" and the new spiritual life which proceeds from him is superinduced upon an animal or earthly nature. Christians are twice born; first by nature, again by Spirit. By the second birth, the soul that was spiritually dead before, begins to live and move in view of God's character, will, and manifested benevolence in Christ. By the first birth every man has the mental and fleshy nature of Adam; by the second birth every believer has in him the spiritual lineaments of Christ. This new divine nature is developed out of the old earthly nature, or superinduced upon it. As the chrysalis has the lineaments of the butterfly within it, while yet it retains the body, and, to some extent, the instincts of the caterpillar, so the Christian has the spiritual lineaments of Christ formed in his soul, while yet he retains the earthly nature of his earthly progenitor. In the resurrection, the spiritual soul, disenthralled from its Adamic corporeity, will assimilate to itself, by divine power, a body of a spiritual nature, adapted to the propensions of its new spiritual life, "fashioned like unto Christ's glorious body." Hence, the "image of Christ formed in the soul" here, is the only "hope of glory" hereafter.

The spiritual and the earthly nature, the one being superinduced upon the other, are antagonistic the one to the other. It is reasonable to suppose that, as in the lipodeptera, the rudiments of the winged insect prevail against the worm from which it is developed, the antagonistic efforts of the two opposing instincts are felt, and the one prevails over the other with a struggle; so, in the case of those who are "born of the Spirit," "the flesh lusteth against the Spirit, and the Spirit against the flesh, and these are contrary the one to the other."

When a man is born again, the two natures are distinctly marked by the diverse aliment upon which they live. The natural mind lives on natural aliment, and seeks its highest good on earth. The spiritual mind grows and develops itself by truth. The new nature draws its life from Christ. The conscience, the affections, and the will, live and move in view of God in Christ. God becomes the spiritual Father of the spiritual soul, and the "new-created" is a son. Truth is eternal; Christ is eternal. Hence, the soul which lives on this aliment has eternal life. Jesus said, "I am the bread of life, of which if a man eat he shall never die, but shall have everlasting life." The natural man "liveth by bread alone," but the Christian liveth "by every word that proceedeth out of the mouth of God."

In the light of this philosophy, which is discriminatingly true to the Scriptures, we may see the reason and the necessity of the doctrine of the divine Spirit. The glory of the gospel is in its power, offered at this point, to transform the human soul from the habitudes of an earthly to that of a spiritual life. A nature cannot transform itself. One species can not produce another. The instincts of the earthly nature can not turn against themselves. The germ of the new nature must be "begotten" in order to prevail against the old. When the new nature is begotten, the old nature becomes as a body of death, until the new rises above it, and brings it into subserviency.

The Scriptures exhibit this subject distinctly. The apostle, in his letter to the Romans, says: "There is, therefore, now no condemnation to them which are in Christ Jesus, who walk not after the flesh, but after the Spirit; for the law of the Spirit of Life in Christ Jesus hath made me free from the law of sin and death. For what the law could not do in that it was weak through the flesh, or because of the earthly nature, God sending his own Son in the likeness of sinful flesh, and for sin, as a sacrifice for sin, condemned sin in the flesh, that the righteousness of the law may be fulfilled in us, who walk, not after the flesh but after the Spirit; i. e. not after the old nature, but the new. For they who have only the earthly nature, 'are earthly,' do interest themselves only in the things of the earth; and they that have the spiritual nature are interested in the things of the Spirit. "For to be carnally-minded is death." Those who are governed only by earthly and selfish motives and aims are spiritually dead. "But to be spiritually-minded is life and peace. For the carnal mind is enmity against God. It is not subject to his law, neither indeed can be." So then, they that are in the flesh, or natural state, can not please God.

"But if the Spirit of him that raised up Jesus Christ from the dead dwell in you, he that raised up Christ from the dead shall also quicken your mortal bodies by his Spirit that dwelleth in you."

Look a moment at one or two of the points in this passage.

The law can give knowledge of duty, but it can not beget life. It can show us the evil, but it can not beget the disposition to overcome the evil. It is not knowledge that men want, but strength to do what they know. The man is a fool who supposes that light is love. The law requires love, but it can not beget it. Every thing begets its kind. Love only can beget love. Hence, Christ crucified in the humanity as a sacrifice for sin, is such an exhibition of love that it begets love in believers. Faith accomplishes "what the law could not do." Love is life. "Love is the fulfilling of the law," and hence "the law of God is fulfilled in us who walk not after the flesh, but after the Spirit." Men by nature are morally "dead already," and have no "eternal life" unless born again by the Spirit of Holiness in Christ Jesus.

In the Christian are the rudiments of a new species, a new and higher type of the rational order of humanity. His new life is by divine interposition, but received in accordance with his own voluntary powers, begotten by truth and cherished by love. The spiritual germ is implanted and developed here until it attains the resurrection state—i. e. overcomes the habitudes of its earthly body; then, in the resurrection, a spiritual body adapted to its propensions is given to it. "To every seed its own adapted body." Christ is the head and the type of the new creation: shall we say of the new species? The process now developing in Christian minds on the earth, will reach, in body and spirit, a glorious consummation in the resurrection of the just.

CHAPTER IX.

RECONCILIATION, OR AT-ONE-MENT.

The Christian doctrine of atonement is held confidingly by the evangelical churches; but, determinedly rejected by skeptical writers, as it is likewise by most of those calling themselves Unitarians.

It should be stated at the outset, that the subject of sacrifice has its essential relations with the moral nature of man—the conscience, the affections, the will—rather than with the intellect. The love-power of sacrifice when appropriated by faith, its relations to man's moral nature, and to God's moral government, are too profound to be fully developed by mere logical elucidation. The sacrifice of Christ is a manifestation of power and love transferred by faith to the consciousness of the believer. The skeptic can not know this. Hence the main evidence is absent in his case. But there are adaptations of the atonement to human susceptibility, there are grounds of its necessity in moral government, which may be seen by the reason; and seeing these, a reason that is reverent will accept the aid of faith which gives us the substance of what the reason had given us by distinct indication.

We inquire, then, is there any thing in the nature of man which is met only by the sacrifice of Christ, offered not for himself, but for those who will accept its mercy by faith?

It can not be doubted that there is in man a consciousness of sin, or of something else, call it what you will, that leads him to feel the want of a sacrifice; or rather that leads him to sacrifice as a means of reconciliation with God. Since the world began man has had something in his soul that has led him to offer sacrifice. We inquire neither for the reason of the fact, nor for the form of the fact, but for the fact itself. Men may call the fact propitiation, expiation, substitution, by any or all these names, still the thing sought by the soul is plain: it is peace with God, a mitigation of the consciousness of sin, reconciliation, at-one-ment. Superstitious usages have been connected with sacrifice, and priestcraft has turned the offering of the sin-oppressed soul to a selfish account; but the preversion of the fact does not ignore the existence of a sense of want in the soul which has produced in all ages and among all nations, the various phenomena of sacrifices.

The ultimate truth in the case, then is, that there is something in the human soul that leads men to seek peace with God by sacrifice. The form may be varied never so much. Some may inflict torture upon themselves; some part with what they deem most precious, even a son or a daughter; some make a pilgrimage; some offer the first-fruits of grain or of cattle. Whatever the form, the phenomena are all produced by the one want of the sin-conscious soul, a desire of peace, or at-one-ment with God.

The want of atonement felt in the soul is as universal as the sense of sin. Man, therefore, as a being, naturally seeks reconciliation by sacrifice, because his reason, as well as his moral sense, teaches him that sin alienates and separates from God.

In this connection notice an important fact, a

fact which is evidence not only of the fallen and darkened state of the human mind, but likewise of the necessity of revelation, especially of the revelation of the mercy of God by sacrifice. While the sense of sin, which is universal, produces in men the sense of want which demands a propitiation, yet to offer self, or suffering, or any object we can call our own, produces selfishness and pride in the soul, instead of benevolence, gratitude, and humility. We feel the want of a sacrifice, but nothing we possess produces the effect necessary in order to peace of conscience and purity of heart. The man who goes upon a pilgrimage to Mecca, or to any other shrine, especially if he walked on his knees a part of the way, returns to his home a censorious and self-righteous spirit, his self-sacrifice having led him away from humility, and rendered gratitude impossible. He can not be grateful to God for a salvation which he himself has worked out for himself. So with the devotee who tortures himself. So in the case of those who give, as a propitiation, money or cattle. The effect necessarily connected with sacrifice, when that sacrifice is made by self for self, is the opposite of that which the sacrifice of Christ for the sinner is adapted to produce. The one produces self-righteousness and self-dependence, the other gratitude and dependence on God.*

This then is the actual condition of man in his natural state. He has a sense of sin, and the accompanying sense of the necessity of sacrifice; but the selfish sacrifices to which his natural want leads, produce evil and not good in the soul. Instead of rendering a man humble and grateful, the sacrifice prompted by the natural want, and offered by self for self, produces pride and impiety. It has done so since the beginning of the world, and would have continued to do so until the end of the world, if divine revelation and divine love had not revealed Christ crucified, which rescues the soul from selfish sacrificing. Skeptics can not deny these facts. If they reject the gospel solution of them, we defy them to furnish any other that does not impugn either the justice or the mercy of God; and thus involve the difficulty in deeper darkness. "The Lamb slain from the foundation of the world," to be "testified to all in due time," is the only solution.

* It is a singular fact that some liberal writers make out, that a "sense of dependence" is the ultimate idea in religion, and yet discard the doctrine which alone produces a sense of dependence.

In what way, then, could the natural want of propitiation be met, and the soul receive spiritual good by the sacrifice?

We have anticipated the answer to this question. But let us look at one or two particulars. In the first place, it is necessary, in order to the formation of a benevolent character, that the motive of our action be out of self. What I do for another's good makes me more benevolent. What I do from selfish motives makes me more selfish. Now the man who has faith in Christ's love-sacrifice for us, is redeemed from a selfish motive. He labors for Christ's sake. Christ's sacrifice moves him. He is God-moved, not self-moved. Christ becomes motive, both in the heart and in the will. Faith produces gratitude and good works, but works can never produce faith.

The sacrifice of Christ then is a necessary part of the moral system which includes man as a sinner. Without it the natural sense of sin and dependence works injury to the human soul. With it the sense of sin in believers is canceled by a sense of reconciliation; and reason and conscience find rest by trust in the divine sacrifice. A sense of dependence, by faith, places the soul in its true position. It depends not on itself, but on the love of God manifested in Christ's sacrifice. And every time we pray in his name, the sense of dependence and gratitude is renewed in the mind.

The introductory dispensation of Moses produced, so far as an initiatory process of types and figures could produce, the salutary ideas which are produced under the Christian dispensation by the sacrifice of Christ.

The faith and ritual of the Mosaic institution was such, that the sacrifice offered was not deemed the property of the individual, but as belonging to the Lord, *Exodus*, 13: 11–16. The Lord permitted the redemption by sacrifice of the first-born, which belonged to him by the most solemn covenant. The ceremonial was such that the offering was to the mind of the Jew, the Lord's sacrifice, while yet it was permitted to be offered in behalf of the sinner, for a sin or a peace-offering. Thus the idea of ownership in the offering was destroyed by the plan of the Mosaic economy; hence, the concomitant idea of pride and self-righteousness could not follow the offering. The fee of the sacrifice was in Jehovah, not in the sinner who offered it.

But as a sense of sin would again arise by renewed transgression or omission of known duty, hence a succession of sacrifices was the burden of the old law. These sacrifices, says the apostle, "could not make the comers thereunto perfect." The renewed sense of sin required a renewed sacrifice. The thing needed to meet the want was one sacrifice that could be pleaded perpetually, which would thus make the comers perfect, and supersede forever the offering of sacrifices by penitent worshipers. Hence the whole system is fulfilled in the sacrifice of Christ. He is "the end of the law, of sacrifice, to every one that believeth." "Nor yet that he should offer himself often, as the high priest entereth into the holy place every year with the blood of others;" *Heb.* 9: 25, "but now once in the end of the dispensation hath he appeared, to put away sin by the sacrifice of himself." Hence, "the blood of Christ, who by the eternal Spirit offered himself without spot unto God, will purge your consciences from dead works to serve the living God."

It is not necessary to inquire, as some have done, whether in the darkness of the age, the divine Father adapted the sacrifices which the natural want had produced, and which were then existing, to the end of initiating the one sacrifice offered by the eternal Spirit, which would more perfectly purify the conscience and heart, and produce obedience by a right motive. It is enough to know the fact that the sacrifice of Christ does purify the heart, does speak peace to the conscience, does redeem the soul from selfish or dead works, and does produce works of love in those who are servants of the living God.

There is another aspect of the atonement which is frequently brought to view in the Scriptures, and which many consider the foundation of its necessity.

Man has an innate sense of justice and right. This is a distinguishing attribute of his moral nature. A sense of responsibility for all moral action of which conscience takes cognizance is based upon it. A sense of the evil and desert of sin arises, in a great measure, from the sense of justice, which is in conflict with sin. Law is the development of justice, as benevolence is the development of love. Now love often develops itself in acts which are superior to law, because they are acts of self-denial which the law, or justice does not demand. But laws are the immutable rules of the creation, physical and moral; and the best exercise of mercy is to aid in bringing the ignorant and erring back to light and law. Justice, then, underlies mercy, and mercy is exercised in maintainance of the principles of eternal justice. Mercy rises above law only to bring back the transgressor into conformity to law.

Now, God having given to man this intuitive sense of justice, would not violate it by atonement or in any other way. Besides, God himself possesses the attribute of justice, and his moral government, even in the administration of mercy, must be based upon it.

The principle of justice then, which develops itself in law can not be sacrificed to the power of mercy which develops itself in benevolence; nor can the one produce the effects which the other does in the human mind. Gratitude can not be exercised fully for an action in others which the law requires them to perform. We must see in the act something of the mercy which is above law, producing acts of personal self-denial for us, before gratitude can flow spontaneously. But the being who, while he maintains the principles of justice, exercises mercy by acts of self-denial which the law does not require, commends himself both to the conscience and the affections of moral beings, and begets in all right minds not only a sense of regard for righteousness, but at the same time a sense of grateful love for him as a benefactor.

There are many who seem to have no right sense of the principles of justice and mercy as they relate to moral government. This state of mind is born of ignorance and sin. God is not only the Father, especially of those who are "born of the Spirit," but he is the ruler and judge of men. A father may pardon a son for an offence against himself; but if he is a magistrate, and that son commits the same offence against the public law, he can not pardon him without forfeiting his character as a ruler, or impairing the sense of justice in the public mind.

If the sense of justice is of God and in God, he will maintain it in moral government. It is necessary as a basis for repentance.

Pardon must be tendered in a form that will produce repentance. A proclamation of pardon on repentance would render repentance a selfish act, or if proclaimed before the act, it would license sin. "God is love," and therefore in governing the world he would exercise benevolence; but benevolence would be exercised in such a manner as to maintain the sense of justice, which is the basis of moral government.

We desire not only to elucidate this subject, but to produce positive conviction in relation to it. Instead of reproducing the same thought, allow me to refer to the chapters on law and atonement in my work. "God Revealed in Creation and in Christ," beginning with the second book, and thence onward to the 198th page.

I commend most heartily the whole subject of law and atonement there set forth. Let them be read with the conviction in mind, that in order to maintain the principle of justice in the minds of intelligent beings, God must develop and maintain this principle in his own moral government. And in connection with this, that benevolence, which is above law, can be governmentally exercised only to bring back transgressors to obedience to law. As law is the only foundation of order in the moral universe, and of safety and happiness to the creature, benevolence can be exercised in no way that is congruous with the system, except by the restoration of offenders, pardoned because transformed from love of sin to God.

This inviolability of moral law finds a sanction in the reason and conscience of men. The moral law is an expression of the will of God. He could not, therefore, permit sin without permitting a violation of his own will, which would be absurd. Besides, if God is holy he ought not to make a law which would permit sin. No man will say that God ought to make a law that would allow a single transgression. Now, if the reason and conscience that God has given men, say, and sanction the saying, that God ought not to permit sin, who dare rebel against his moral nature, and say that he has done so? Reason affirms, conscience sanctions, and the moral law reveals the same penalty that is written against the transgressor of every other law of the universe—The transgressing subject shall die.

How, then, shall man be restored and pardoned? How shall the evil propension be eradicated, and the evil he had occasioned in others be balanced and compensated for? Is there any method by which—without impairing the sense of justice—benevolence, which is above law, may restore the transgressor to obedience, and arrest the evils which his sin has occasioned in other minds. This is the problem of the atonement, viewed in the light of law, and of the solidarity of mankind.

You will understand what I mean when I apply this philosophical term to the human races. It is as true of the human family as of any other family in natural history. The phrases of the New Testament, in regard to sin and salvation, assume, in many passages, the idea of the solidarity of mankind. A true exposition of the atonement can not be given without taking this doctrine into account. "As in Adam all died, so in Christ shall all be made alive." First, the natural—then the spiritual. The latter counteracting the former; and God over all.

There are, in the physical universe, compensations which are placed over against each other; and thus the inequalities of the various parts of a system are met and balanced. These compensations or adjustments are made by the Creator; and they become at once the evidences of his wisdom and goodness. Notice!

1. The moral law, which requires supreme love to God and impartial love to man, is the rule of reason and righteousness; and being the will of God, it is the obligatory law for all intelligent and moral beings. From this statement I presume there will be no dissent.

2. Now, accepting the law as the rule of life, it is admitted that man falls below its requirements; that, judged by the law, he is condemned as a transgressor. He is guilty in view of his own conscience, knowledge, and ability. He is likewise guilty in nature, or in character, not having the disposition to fulfill his duties according to the example of Christ. The penalties of the law are therefore against him, and he can neither pardon himself nor beget that love in himself which is the fulfilling of the law.

3. Now, is there any compensation in the moral universe for this aberration of man from the sphere of law? Is there a recuperative principle in the moral as there is in the physical system of things? Is there a redeeming power adapted to the nature of the case? Let us see!

The thing required in order to moral compensation is that some being or beings united in the same system with man, should possess a moral worth rising above law in the same degree that man falls below it, and that this worth should complement want of love by increase of love.

Now, we postulate that Jesus Christ, by his sacrifice, meets this condition in the equation. The law can not demand the sacrifice of the innocent for the guilty. Its requirement can rise no higher than perfect obedience. The death ot Christ, therefore, was above law; and if it tended to honor the law by restoring transgressors to obedience, it accomplished on one side an actual balance against what was deficient on the other side.

The question, then, of vital interest is, does the super-merit of Christ, which is above law, practically counterwork the demerit of man, which is below law? Now, we affirm that this result is actually and practically accomplished in every one that believes in the divine sacrifice of the Redeemer for his sin.

"Love is the fulfilling of the law." Christ's sacrifice was a love-sacrifice, a sacrifice produced by divine love. The law required obedience, but could not produce it. It required love, but could not beget love. The sacrifice of Christ is a revealment of divine love, and hence, as every thing begets its kind, by the love of God manifest in Christ, love for God in Christ is begotten in believers.

"If men love God, they will keep his commandments." Hence the disposition to obedience is restored in the soul of every one who believes in Christ; so that the current of death which originated in Adam is met and counteracted by the current of life which originated in Christ. One was made a "living soul," that is, an earthly being, the other is a "quickening," that is, life-giving Spirit.

Faith in Christ disposes men to love and obey him. It produces peaceful obedience in the soul; it casts out sin; it works by love, and purifies the heart.

What then, is the thing which constitutes the merit and power of the divine sacrifice? We answer, its merit is in its love, which is above law. Its personal suffering endured for others. This fact likewise constitutes its power. I can not love with the love of gratitude one who does no more for me than the law requires him to do. But when love transcends law, and one rescues me by a sacrifice of himself, a sacrifice which love prompted, but which law did not require, then my heart, and the heart of every believer responds by grateful love to the Redeemer. Thus "faith works by love," and love works by obedience, and affectionate obedience is restoration and salvation.

The merit, then, is found in the sacrifice of Christ, which, as an expression of divine love, restores the transgressor and procures pardon by fitting him for pardon in the sight of the law. By this merit—not his own—the sinner can be pardoned, while by its power he is turned from sin, and restored to obedience.

Thus death and life are both recognized in the divine government; and Christ came in our humanity "to give himself a ransom for many," "that whosoever believeth might not perish but have eternal life."

And finally, the doctrine of atonement, as held by experienced Christians, meets the deepest sense of want in the soul. It produces a sense of dependence, humility, and love to God, and has given hope and joy, in life and in death, to Christian hearts in all ages.

Now adaptation is from God. God can not produce holiness of heart by a falshood. Truth is known by its effects. As God is true, that which glorifies God and does good to man at the same time, is truth; therefore the evangelical view of the atonement is truth.

CHAPTER X.

ON FUTURE RETRIBUTION.

Liberal Christians frequently refer to the subject of future retribution, but do not often announce their own opinions. There are passages, however, in which they speak distinctly. Such for instance as "the woes of sin are its antidote. Suffering comes from wrong-doing, as well-being from virtue. If there be suffering in the next world, it is, as in this, but the medicine of the sickly soul." *

This is plain. Mr. Parker adopted the opinions of those who are called Universalists on the subject of future retribution. He is wiser than those generally are who think with him. He affirms without argument. Others argue, and in their argument reason sees the fallacy.

We can but doubt the sincerity of men who profess to find their religion in the Bible, and

* Theodore Parker's Discourse, Page 438.

yet tell us they believe in no future punishment. The Bible can not be interpreted to favor such views except by subterfuge and perversion on the part of the interpreter. Mr. Parker, therefore, seldom refers to the Bible on this subject. There is at least frankness in the audacity of the skeptic who sets his own reason above the reason of the Bible, and rejects or modifies it when it does not accord with his own conceptions. But to assume that the Bible is in agreement with the doctrine of "no future punishment," is a subterfuge that "perverts the right ways of the Lord," and indicates dishonesty in the interpreter.

We shall give the more attention to this subject, because it is one of vital interest to all persons who enjoy the light of the gospel. It has to do with the motives which deter men from sin. We do not say that Christians act in view of future retribution. Love deters the Christian from sin. For him there is no evil in the future. But for the unthankful and disobedient—for those who abuse the divine mercy and harden themselves in selfishness, there is evil in the future; and repentance with such is impossible so long as they believe there is no future punishment. Convince an impenitent man that sin will not exclude him from future happiness; that all the evil he will experience is present inconvenience or compunction of conscience, and with such convictions, repentance toward God and faith in our Lord Jesus Christ are out of the question. Every wicked man is willing to take the sin with its present evil; and as for the figment, that the consequences of sin will cure sin, or remove the cause of sinning, it is, as we shall see further on, contrary to both reason and the Scriptures.

An argument for error is destroyed so soon as its fallacy is made apparent. The Universalist view of the future state, which many liberalists hold, can be shown to be erroneous both in reason and Scripture. We shall endeavor to make this apparent, and to reach, by our conclusion, the evil not only as it is maintained by Universalists, but as it prevails in a wider sense.

You will notice that in this and succeeding chapters, and indeed in all I have written on this subject, I use the Scripture phrases, without discussing the questions at issue between denominations, in relation to what will be the character of future punishment. I make no effort to determine the mode of punishment, whether it be to sin and suffer forever, or whether the "second death" be the death of the soul. Archbishop Whately and others have discussed those points. We argue only the question at issue with Universalists and those who, like them, believe in no future punishment; or, if there be any, that it is only disciplinary. We do not wish to occupy space with any other issue than the main one. The main question is not whether "God will destroy the soul and body of the wicked in hell?" or whether he will permit them to live sinning and suffering forever. The negative of the position that all men will be saved, is, that all men will not be saved. We believe this point is plain, whether we view it in the light of reason or of revelation. The other question concerning eternal sin and suffering, or the destruction of those unfitted for heaven, admits of discussion, and whichever way it may be settled by any one, the vital doctrines of the Scripture remain intact. In either case, the finally impenitent never enter the kingdom of the blessed.

In all discussions relating to this subject I use Scriptural phrases. These prove that those who die unregenerated will "never see life." Whether they will be annihilated after the judgment, or sin and suffer forever, we leave for scholars and sincere inquirers to determine.

We are aware that the intensity and eternity of future misery have sometimes been urged with a spirit which indicated any thing else in the polemic beside a sense of the merciful character of God. Advantage has been taken of this to create prejudice against evangelical piety, and to destroy in the minds of those who disobey the gospel the salutary impression that without repentance, they will be "reserved unto the day of judgment to be punished."

Let us leave, then, whatever may be doubtful or difficult concerning the mere form of the doctrine of future punishment, and consider the main proposition, that neither Scripture nor reason teach the future salvation of those who die impenitent; but that they will "perish" in the "second death," whatever that second death may be.

Notice, first, the insincerity of any effort which seeks to derive the doctrine of no future punishment from the Scriptures. By skillful perversion, Universalism might be tortured out of Bunyan, or Baxter, or Edwards, much more readily than it can be out of the Bible. By the same artifice universal damnation may be proved, the one as readily as the other. See this in the following tables—

Universal salvation proved by perverting the Scriptures.	*Universal damnation proved by perverting the Scriptures.*
1st. John, 1: 9. God is faithful and just to forgive us our sins: and to cleanse us from all unrighteousness.	Joshua, 34: 19. He is a holy God, He is a jealous God, He will not forgive your transgressions nor your sins.
Lam. 3: 31. For the Lord will not cast off forever.	1st Chron. 28: 9. If thou seek Him, He will be found of thee ; but if thou forsake Him, He will cast thee off forever.
All will be saved, because the Scriptures say, Mal., 2: 10. "Have we not all one father? Hath not one God created us?	All will be damned, because the Scriptures say—Isaiah, 27: 11: He that made them will not have mercy on them ; and He that formed them will show them no favor.
The world will be saved, because the Bible says, Christ gives eternal life to as many as the Father hath given him; and in another place it says, the Father hath put all things into his hands, so that the proof is clear that all will be saved in Christ.	The world will be damned, because the Bible says—They who have not the spirit of Christ are none of His ; and in another place it says positively, the world can not receive the spirit of Christ—therefore it follows that the whole world must inevitably be damned.
All men will be saved, because the Bible teaches that Christ will reconcile all things unto Himself—Col. 1: 20, and says in another place that we	All men will be damned, because the Bible teaches, Jude 15 that the Lord cometh with ten thousand of His saints to execute judgment upon all ; and if

"see not now all things reconciled," implying that all will be reconciled hereafter. Here is universal reconciliation and salvation plainly proved.

we do not see judgment executed upon all now, yet the passage says, the Lord cometh, or will come, to execute judgment on all hereafter.

Again, the words "forever," "everlasting," "forever and ever," occur frequently in the Scriptures, sometimes in connection with temporal, sometimes with spiritual subjects. An attempt has always been made by those who hold the views of Drs. Rider, Chapin, and others, to strip these words of their usual import, which is that of endless duration. Sometimes, as all know, they are applied to temporal things, when the common sense of the reader, as in all other similar cases, will limit them by the nature of the subject. "The everlasting hills" will stand while time lasts; God and the soul live when time dies. When these words are limited in signification, the limitation grows out of the nature of the subject. To this all agree; and this is all that is necessary to show the futility of the effort to destroy their import in connection with the future destiny of the wicked.

THE WORD "EVERLASTING" APPLIED TO EXPRESS THE DURATION OF THE

Happiness of the Righteous.

Matth. 19: 29. Those that leave all to follow Christ, shall "receive an hundred-fold, and shall inherit everlasting life.

Misery of the wicked.

2 Thess. 1: 8, 9. The Lord Jesus shall be revealed from heaven, in flaming fire, taking vengeance on them that know

not God, and obey not the gospel of our Lord Jesus Christ, who shall be punished with everlasting destruction from the presence of the Lord and the glory of His power.

Luke, 18: 30. They "shall receive manifold more in this present time, and in the world to come, life everlasting.

Romans, 6: 22. But now being made free from sin, and become servants of God, ye have your fruit unto holiness, and the end, everlasting life.

Matth. 25: 41. Depart from me, ye cursed, into everlasting fire, prepared for the devil and his angels.

Matth. 18: 8. If thy hand or thy foot offend thee, cut them off and cast them from thee ; it is better for thee to enter into life halt or maimed, rather than having two hands or two feet to be cast into everlasting fire.

Dan. 12: 2. Many of them which sleep in the dust of the earth shall awake, some to everlasting life, and some to shame and everlasting contempt.

Matth. 25: 46. These shall go away into everlasting punishment, but the righteous into life everlasting.

Dan. 12: 2. Many of them which sleep in the dust of the earth shall awake, some to everlasting life, and some to shame and everlasting contempt.

Matth. 25: 46. These shall go away into everlasting punishment, but the righteous into life everlasting.

THE PHRASE "FOREVER AND EVER" AS APPLIED TO EXPRESS THE DURATION OF THE

Happiness of the Righteous.

Dan. 12: 3. They that turn many to righteousness shall shine as stars forever and ever.

Rev. 22: 5. The Lord God giveth them light, and they shall reign forever and ever.

Misery of the Wicked.

Rev. 14: 11. The smoke of their torment ascendeth up forever and ever, and they have no rest day nor night.

Rev. 20: 10. The devil, the beast, and the false prophet shall be tormented day and night forever and ever

Mark, now, we do not argue from these tables that either the existence of punishment or of happiness is eternal. This evangelical christians mostly, think as clear as language can reveal it; but this is not our argument. Our proposition is, that the destruction of the wicked will be as enduring as the happiness of the righteous, because both are supported by precisely the same proof. If liberal christians affirm that these words never mean eternal duration, then they get rid of everlasting punishment; but they likewise get rid of the everlasting God, and of the everlasting life of the righteous.

If they say that they sometimes mean eternal duration, and sometimes limited duration—that the duration is to be inferred from the nature of the subject to which they are applied; then the subject to which they are applied is the same in both cases, man, or the soul of man, or the body of man—whatever they may choose to call the subject, there is no doubt but that it is the same in both cases.

If they reject both of these, and argue that the words "everlasting," and "eternal," and "forever," do not apply to the soul, but to the punishment or misery of the soul or body: then, on the other hand, the words do not apply to the soul of the righteous, but to the happiness or joy of the soul or body; and if misery is not eternal in its nature, then joy or happiness is not eternal in its nature.

Now, whatever these words mean in one case, they mean the same in the other. One thing, therefore, is manifest, namely, that the "death" of the wicked will endure as long as the "life" of the righteous. This truth is as obvious as it is in the proposition that six and half a dozen are equal. If the rule be shortened or lengthened, it must be applied to both sides of the question.

If the Liberalist can succeed in proving that the death of the wicked will end; he has at the same time proved that the life of the righteous will end; because precisely the same words and phrases used to express the one are used to express the other. Thus the dilemma is perfect, and one from which there is no possible escape—that so fast and so far as the liberalist is able to destroy, in the minds of the wicked, the fear of everlasting punishment, he destroys at the same time, in the minds of all that believe him, the hope of everlasting happiness; because the proof which sustains the one is the same that sustains the other; so that if one fails, both fail—if one stands, both stand—and the duration of the one must remain the same as the duration of the other. Thus, like blind Samson in the temple of the uncircumcised Philistines, if Universalists could succeed in subverting the pillars of the temple of truth, the wreck would fall upon the heads of their audience.

There are but two ways by which it is possible to express truth in language. The same truth may be asserted affirmatively and negatively, and when a proposition is proved affirmatively and negatively, it is not possible to make it either stronger or plainer.

Now, the "everlasting punishment" of the impenitent is not only, as proved above, repeatedly affirmed in the word of God, but it is likewise asserted in a negative form, a form by which the existence of God and the happiness of the righteous are also expressed. In relation to God it is written, "Thy dominion shall not pass away." In relation to the righteous, they shall receive "a crown of glory that fadeth not away." In relation to the wicked, consider the following:

"He that believeth not the Son shall not see life, but the wrath of God abideth on him."

The blasphemy against the Holy Ghost "shall not be forgiven unto men, neither in this world, neither in the world to come."

"In hell he lifted up his eyes, being in torment." "Between us and you there is a great gulf fixed, so that those who would pass from hence to you can not, neither can they pass to us who would come from thence."

"Their worm dieth not, and their fire is not quenched."

"Without holiness no man shall see the Lord."

"For if ye believe not that I am he ye shall die in your sins."

The truth in relation to this topic is, that the same words which are applied in the Bible to teach the eternity of God and the eternity of happiness, are applied to teach the eternity of that "destruction" which shall come upon the wicked. They are the strongest words and phrases which can be used in any langnage; and all competent interpreters agree that their first import is eternal. And in addition to this, the same truth is taught not only affirmatively but negatively; so that the everlasting punishment of the wicked is proved in the strongest way, and in all the ways that human language can prove any truth.

Universalists adopt a peculiar method of interpretation in order to escape the force of the figurative language used in the New Testament. Because the figures which relate to future punishment had a local and temporal origin, they infer that they have only a local and temporal import. The word translated hell they find originally referred to the valley of the sons of Hinnom, near Jerusalem; hence they confine the figure to its fact, and thus destroy the end for which figures were made. Dr. Clarke has not told us whether he adopts the reasoning of those who believe with him in this matter, but as he adopts their conclusions, it is fair to infer he adopts their reasons. Now, if the force of figures is to be destroyed on one side of the argument, it should be on the other; then, supposing this reasoning to be true, there is neither a heaven nor a hell. The word heaven is derived from a word which in its original import signified the atmosphere or the firmament; and the import of the word paradise is a garden. In both cases the words which signify heaven and hell are educed from things temporal and local in their nature. If one must be divested of its meaning, which signifies a state of future punishment, then the other must be divested of its import, which signifies a state of future happiness. We should then, according to this method of interpretation, have neither a hell nor a heaven.

This interpretation strikes at the foundation of revelation. It would be impossible, if such perversions were permitted, for any revelation ever to be made to man. Man can learn the unknown only by figures and parables drawn from the known:

> "For what of God above or man below?
> What can we reason but from what we know?"

No terms are used in the Bible to teach us the existence of a future world, or the condition of the soul in that world, which are not derived in some way from things that pertain to the present state of existence. The Saviour always spake in parables and figures, Matt. 13: 34, because He had to illustrate the unknown by what was known to His hearers. The individual, therefore, who endeavors to destroy in the minds of his hearers the application of these figures to another life, destroys, so far as he succeeds, the very effect which Christ designed to accomplish by using them. This method of interpretation proves there is no hell, but it proves, likewise, that there is no devil, no angel, no heaven, no God!

The general tenor of the New Testament—the general acceptation of the words and phrases used by Christ and His apostles, as well as the effects produced by their ministry, render it certain that they taught men that eternal life depended on reconciliation to God as He is manifested in Jesus Christ. Notice the evidence of this in the following passages.

The points of these passages can not be misunderstood. "Fear not them which kill the body, but are not able to kill the soul, but rather fear him which is able to destroy both soul and body in hell."

John, 5; 25—29. "Marvel not at this, for the hour is coming in which all that are in their graves shall hear His voice; and shall come forth they that have done good unto the resurrection of life; and they that have done evil unto the resurrection of damnation."

The judgment is, by the sacred writers, put in order after death, and the resurrection of the dead.

Heb. 6: 2. "The doctrine of baptisms, and

of the laying on of hands, and of the resurrection of the dead, and of eternal judgment."

Heb. 9: 27. "And as it is appointed unto men once to die, but after this the judgment; so Christ was once offered, or died once, and unto them which look for Him, shall He appear the second time, without sin unto salvation."

2 Tim. 4: 7, 8. "I have fought a good fight, I have finished my course, I have kept the faith; henceforth there is laid up for me a crown of righteousness, which the Lord, the righteous judge, will give me at that day; and not to me only, but unto all them also that love His appearing." Was this righteous judgment when Paul would be crowned with "all that loved Christ's appearing," or "all them that looked for Him" to be at the destruction of Jerusalem? Or was it then taking place? Either idea is an absurdity.

2 Tim. 4: 1. "I charge thee, therefore, before God and the Lord Jesus Christ, who shall judge the quick, [living] and the dead, at His appearing and His kingdom."

2 Pet. 2: 7. "But the heavens and the earth which are now, by the same word are kept in store, reserved unto fire, against the day of judgment and perdition of ungodly men."

By looking at the preceding verses it will be seen that Peter is speaking of the physical earth, affirming its destruction or dissolution once by water, and its final change or dissolution by fire; at which time will be the day of judgment and the "perdition of ungodly men." Observe, he says the present earth is "kept in store, reserved unto fire against the day of judgment and perdition of ungodly men." How could language make the truth plainer, that the day of judgment and perdition of ungodly men will be at the time when this earth shall be changed by fire?

2 Pet. 2: 4, 9. "The Lord knoweth how to deliver the godly out of temptation, and to reserve the unjust unto the day of judgment, to be punished."

Mark, the unjust are punished as they go along, and reserved besides unto, not a day, nor this day, nor all days, but the day of judgment, to be punished.

Matt. 12: 32. "Whosoever speaketh a word against the Son of man, it shall be forgiven him. But whosoever speaketh against the Holy Ghost, it shall not be forgiven him, neither in this world nor in the world to come."

John, 3: 16. "For God so loved the world that He gave His only-begotten Son, that whosoever believeth in Him should not perish, but have everlasting life." If this does not imply that whosoever does not believe in Him shall perish and not have everlasting life, then there is no meaning in language.

John, 6: 54. "Whosoever eateth my flesh and drinketh my blood hath eternal life, and I will raise him up at the last day." What does this imply, unless Christ deceived His disciples?

Acts, 24: 25. "And as Paul reasoned of righteousness, temperance, and judgment to come Felix trembled." Was it a judgment that had already come, or the destruction of Jerusalem, that had made a Roman governor tremble?

1 Peter, 4: 18. "And if the righteous scarcely be saved, where shall the ungodly and the sinner appear?" Easily answered, says this doctrine. They will appear in heaven, with the righteous who are scarcely saved.

Matt: 26, 24. "It had been good for that man if he had not been born." How could this be, if Judas went to heaven at death? If the doctrine of Universalist preachers be true, Judas got to heaven before Jesus.

"He with a cord outwent his Lord,
And got to heaven first."

Luke, 10: 42. "But one thing is needful, and Mary hath chosen that good part that shall never be taken away from her." Will those who do not choose it have the good part and the one thing needful, which shall never be taken away from them?

James, 1: 15. "Then when lust hath conceived, it bringeth forth sin: and sin, when it is finished, bringeth forth death. The liberalist says, sin works its own cure, that when sin is finished it brings forth life. Which is right?

John, 8: 51. "Verily, verily, I say unto you, (mark it,) if a man keep my sayings he shall never see death." Does this mean the first or the second death—death of the body, or of the soul?

It is not doubted by any well-informed person that Christ and His apostles used the words and phrases which those who heard them—those to whom they wrote—would understand as teaching the future punishment of the wicked. They either taught what they believed on this subject, or they willfully deceived the people. They not only used the words which the Jews used to designate future punishment, but they were even careful that the Gentiles should not mistake their meaning. Hence Paul speaks of "blackness of darkness," and Peter uses the word "Tartarus" to convey the same idea.

The whole form and pressure of the apostolic teaching represent themselves and those who heard them as acting under a deep sense of responsibility in regard to the future. "We must all stand before the judgment-seat of Christ." "Knowing the terrors of the Lord, we persuade men." They "warned every man night and day with tears."

Some who heard them "trembled;" others cried out "Men and brethren, what shall we do?" And believers took up their cross daily and followed Christ—all of them to persecution, and many of them to the flames. Does liberal preaching have this effect?

Now, I do not know that a vindication of the Scriptures is necessary, yet there may be those that it may save from a leap into the darkness of skepticism; and we offer this vindication of the Scriptures as a basis of the rational exposition which will ensue.

CHAPTER XI.

REFUTATION OF COMMON FALLACIES ON THE SUBJECT OF FUTURE RETRIBUTION.

We are told, as noticed in a preceding chapter that "the woes of sin are but its antidote. Suffering comes from wrong-doing, as well-being from virtue. If there be suffering in the next world, it is, as in this, but the medicine for the sickly soul."

In the above sentence the usual method is adopted. Truth is adroitly mingled with error. The fallacy of disciplinary punishment, as a cure for sin, and the hope of universal salvation, is propagated in a form of words which, in proper connections, would teach a general truth. All good men believe that "suffering comes from wrong-doing, as well-being from virtue;" but it does not therefore follow that the woes of sin are its antidote, either in this world or the next.

It is true, no doubt, that good men are afflicted for their sins in this world; their discipline produces reform, and fits them for heaven. But it does not follow that the woes of sin produce the same effect upon the impenitent mind. Such a result in the case of those who are not converted is impossible, because it is only by the exercise of faith that discipline from God becomes a good in the soul. In the case of those who have faith, a Father's hand and a Father's love are seen in adverse providences. They receive them as discipline, and are brought by them into a penitent and filial temper; and thus temporal afflictions are, as a matter of experience, a means of separating a believing mind from evil. But in the case of those who are "without faith and without God in the world," temporal afflictions do not produce piety. God does not design to reform sinners by the woes of sin. If he does, he fails in his object; because some men sin, and suffer the woes of sin all their lives, and grow worse and worse till they die. If, therefore, God disciplines them in order to reform them, the effort is worse than a failure, because instead of making them better, it makes them worse.

It is not only a fact which all but the morally blind can see, that the discipline which is a "savor of life unto life" with some, is a "savor of death unto death" with others: but it is likewise a distinctly revealed doctrine of the New Testament: "God knows how to deliver the godly out of temptation, and to reserve the unjust unto the day of judgment to be punished." The inspired writer says to his fellow-Christians, "When we are afflicted we are chastened of the Lord, that we may not be condemned with the world." So far, then, as this world is concerned, it is matter of experience and of revelation that while the woes of sin are a moral discipline and a moral benefit to one class, they do not benefit the other.

That wicked and worldly men often repent when they feel the consequences of their wrongdoing, there is no doubt. But selfish repentance "worketh death." Instead of making men better, it makes them worse. They sorrow because they have injured themselves. Such repentance is selfish, and fits men for hell. "The sorrow of the world worketh death." The effects of sinning upon selfish minds make them worse instead of better; and so far as preachers lead unregenerated men to believe that the woes they experience in consequence of their sins will be a cure of sin, they aid to fit them for the "second death." These are solemn words, but they are true.

Now, without dwelling further on the philosophical blunder, which any thoughtful mind should be ashamed to commit, i.e. that an effect will change or cure its cause, let me invite your attention to another aspect in which this doctrine perverts the right ways of the Lord. If suffering be the medicine that cures sin, then pain cures the disease. Suffering is the effect and evidence of derangement, physical and moral, and in itself tends to death, not to life. It is likewise, declaratory of derangement, and admonishes to seek a remedy.

Instead of sin being a self-destructive, it is a self-strengthening and self-perpetuating principle. Instead of the consequences of a sinful act tending to cure the sinful propension, it actually strengthens it. After one sin, another is more easily and more readily committed; because the sinful act weakens the conscience, confirms a sinful habit, and strengthens the propension to sin in the soul. As a matter of fact, sin blinds the moral vision, and kills the moral sense. The more sinful any individual becomes, the less he sees and the less he feels of the evil of sin. This momentous moral fact can not be denied. It is a natural law—the law of divine judgment, and so long as it is true, the statement that the effect of sinning cures sin is a fallacy uttered in the face of law, experience, and the Scriptures.

The doctrine that conscience punishes men for sin is an impeachment of the justice of God. If this were true, in order that God might be just, the greatest sinner should be the greatest sufferer. But the opposite of this is true. A good man will suffer more for neglecting his prayers, than a bad one will feel for the crime of profaneness. If conscience is the measure of God's justice, then the divine being loves the wicked more than He loves the good; because the more holy the mind, the more potent is conscience—the less holy, the less the infliction. If "men are punished as they go along," and suffer in this world in proportion to their sin, then, as we have said before, Jesus Christ was the greatest of sinners, because He was the greatest of sufferers.

The fact that conscience dies as sin increases, but grows strong in proportion to holiness, shows, by human experience, what is affirmed in the Scriptures, that the good are punished in this world, while the evil are reserved unto the day of judgment to be punished.

"But," says our philosopher, "suffering comes from wrong-doing, as well-being from virtue." Now, if this fact renders it doubtful whether there be any future punishment, it renders it doubtful, in the same measure, whether there be any future happiness. If sin punishes itself, virtue rewards itself. And if sin ceases to punish itself at death, then virtue ceases to reward itself at death; so that there are neither rewards nor punishments—neither a hell nor a heaven in the life to come.

Let us look, in conclusion, at some facts which are connected with the subject of sin and retribution:—What are the effects of sin in this life? and, do, the effects of sin continue in the future world?

The answers to these inquiries are plain both from reason and the Scriptures. Sin produces two results in the soul. It produces present evil, while at the same time it fits the character for future retribution. Just as benevolent action produces peace and complacency of soul in the present life, and forms the soul into a benevolent character, which fits it for heaven. Every one knows, or ought to know, that while sin produces more or less unrest when the act is done; it likewise, by the same act, fixes character. Like a stream which, running constantly over a rock, wears for itself a channel from which in the end it can not escape, so the soul, by continued action of a selfish or sensual nature, forms a habit which fixes its mode of action for the future. Now, destiny depends upon character. A benevolent heart is happy in its own exercises; a selfish mind is confirming a character which destroys happiness, or rather which renders happiness impossible. All men act either from a selfish motive or a benevolent one. Every selfish act confirms a selfish character, and the man who dies having confirmed a selfish character by a selfish life, is fitted for hell; and as death is not a change of the soul but a change of the body, he will experience evil forever, unless God annihilate him after the judgment.

Is it said now, as a final fallacy that so soon as the soul is separated from sense, and experiences in the next world the evil consequences of sin, these evil consequences will lead to repentance. We answer that repentance in view of the experience of evil or the fear of evil, is repentance toward self, not toward God. The more men repent from an experience of evil consequences, the more they are damned. The thief always repents when the sheriff arrests him. The approach of death forces many men to submit, others to repent. Such repentance is by necessity, or in view of consequences, not in view of God's goodness and of the evil of sin. Some weak people talk of repentance on the gallows. Dying sinners and murderers repent, but it is a repentance forced upon them in view of the termination of their lives. In this world "repentance toward God" works by reformation; and faith in our Lord Jesus Christ works by love. In the world of doom, or when moral probation is ended, repentance comes by necessity and works by remorse; and faith by trembling. "The devils believe in one God and tremble."

Character is the only hope of heaven. Character that begins with "repentance unto life," and is formed by benevolent aspiration and action—character which is conformed to the divine law, and governed by benevolent motive—which motive is begotten only by faith in God, as manifested in Christ Jesus.

The last thought in the foregoing paragraph brings us to a vital point in the divine process of human salvation. It introduces Christ as the saving power, without which the soul is destitute of divine life. It will admit of a homily, which we will give in conclusion.

"For Christ's sake," is only another expression for the great truth, that all our holy motions and emotions are dependent on Jesus. "In Christ's name" is a recognition that God is manifest in His sacrifice for sin, and that it is in His mercy alone that we have hope. In the solar system there are two motions of subordinate bodies, one on their own axis, the other around the central orbit; so it is in the spiritual world, the renewed soul is self-moved, and moves likewise in its orbit of dependence on God. To feel reliance on the merit of Christ, to trust in His name, binds the soul to the central life, and is the expression of this actual and practical relation. The man who does not feel it moves only on his own axis, and is dead to God, while he lives to self.

Thus the mind that draws its motive from Christ is a restored spirit. The affinity between the divine and human mind is re-united, and the soul takes on its eternal movement around the infinite center of life and love, forever. "O the depth of the riches both of the wisdom and knowledge of God!"

O, holy One, who hath manifested thy mercy to us in Christ Jesus, in thy name and in thy merit we trust for motive to move our will, mercy to affect our heart, and for grace to pardon our sin; and not unto us, but unto thee, be the glory.

CHAPTER XII.

WRITTEN REVELATION A NECESSITY IN ORDER TO THE MORAL DEVELOPMENT AND MORAL PROGRESS OF MANKIND.

Rationalists and skeptics generally, hold that reason, including intuitional and reflective reason, is a sufficient guide for men in matters relating to God. We can not see how men who are conversant with human history, some of whom have made philosophy a study, can adopt such an opinion. The highest result that reason can give on this subject has been worked out in such a variety of circumstances, that a man who fails to learn a lesson that all experience teaches, must have a will over which reason has, in some measure, lost its influence.

The testimony of universal experience is, that all men have an idea of the existence of God, but not of the character of God. Men can not have an intuition of the character of God, for the plain reason that a knowledge of character implies comparison of qualities, and hence requires a process of reason. It is a shallow fallacy in philosophy, that assumes, as many do, that men have an innate idea of the character as well as the being of God. The moral duties of men to each other may be learned in a good measure by experience, even up to the measure of the golden rule. I know the effect which the conduct of another has upon myself. I judge of that conduct, whether it is in itself right or wrong; and hence, by this process, I can determine what would be right in my neighbor's case, were our circumstances changed. Reason is clouded in men, and it is developed slowly in nations; hence, while rules of human morality may be developed by reason, yet it is only in the best ages and in the highest minds that these higher moral conceptions have appeared. But the character of God and the duties of man to his Maker, are different things. Man without faith has no immediate experience of the Divine character, and having a mixed experience by Providence, it is absolutely impossible for reason to clothe the idea of God with the moral attributes which belong to the divine nature.

Now, the universal experience of nations and races of men has certified these facts. The highest attainment of reason in relation to God has been skepticism, or diversity. This was the result in India, in Greece, in Rome, in France, in Germany, and in America. In all ages and nations which have furnished an opportunity for the ultimate development of the reason, the results have been the same.

Greece gathered all the gods of all nations into her capital city. This was the ultimatum of human reason, in the direction of variety. Her philosophers believed in a divine being; but, while they doubted of all the idolatries of the people, they differed as much among themselves as the people did in relation to prevalent superstitions. Such was also the development in Rome. Tully and others expressed the ultimatum of reason in the affirmation, that all things in relation to the gods and the future world were matters of doubt.

Reason reached the same ultimatum in France and Germany. Revelation in those countries was either forbidden are perverted. The people followed the prevailing superstition, while the philosophers reached a skepticism that was malignant and terrible in its effects on human character and human happiness; so terrible, that the people who had been seduced by it, were glad to take refuge again in the stronghold of the old Catholic superstition, as the least of two evils.

The highest result that reason could attain, unaided by revelation, and aided by all the light and experience of past ages, was wrought out fairly in France. It was a complete triumph of skepticism. Every thing concerning God, and man, and the future was involved in utter doubt. Reason triumphed, and ultimated in the worship of herself, in the form of a profligate woman. Reason even doubted her own affirmations; and only enough of light was left to see the darkness into which she had plunged.

This the best minds of the age stated, in words full of true and solemn portent—words which should teach others to recede from the abyss into which these skeptical philosophers looked before they fell.*

* Diderot, dying after a life of doubt and disappointment, said to friends that stood by his couch to close his eyes in the last sleep, "I am about to take a leap in the dark."

In Great Britain and America skepticism can not become so prevalent, because in these countries Christianity is better understood; and where skepticism does prevail, it will seek to attach to itself many of the virtues which Christianity has introduced: but the result of the unguided

The justly-celebrated Rousseau uttered a striking description of the results of skepticism, and the moral character and aim of skeptics. It is true to life, and true for all time—a picture of the highest product of reason unaided by revelation.

He said:

"I have consulted our philosophers, I have perused their books, I have examined their several opinions. I have found them all proud, positive, and dogmatizing, even in their pretended skepticism, knowing every thing, proving nothing, and ridiculing one another; and this is the only point in which they concur, and in which they are right. Daring when they attack, they defend themselves without vigor. If you consider their arguments, they have none but for destruction; if you count their number, each one is reduced to himself; they never unite but to dispute; to listen to them was not the way to relieve myself from my doubts. I conceive that the insufficiency of the human understanding was the first cause of this prodigious diversity of sentiment, and that pride was the second. If our philosophers were able to discover truth, which of them would interest himself about it? Each of them knows that his system is not better established than the others; but he supports it because it is his own: there is not one among them who, coming to distinguish truth from falsehood, would not prefer his own error to the truth that is discovered by another. Where is the philosopher who, for his own glory, would not willingly deceive the whole human race? Where is he who, in the secret of his heart, proposes any other object than his own distinction? Provided he can but raise himself above the commonalty, provided he can eclipse his competitor, he has reason can in no circumstances be any thing better than doubt, varied in its form by the diversity of the different minds that propagate it. Which one of the English skeptics agreed with another in respect to the character of God or human duty? * Who agrees with Parker or Emerson in America? No one ever did or ever can. Skeptics agree in doubt, but they can not agree concerning the things about which they doubt. The effort to propound any thing positive is, in all cases, a failure; and in most cases, as in Priestley's form of worship and

reached the summit of his ambition. The great thing for him is to think differently from other people. Among believers he is an atheist, among atheists a believer. Shun, shun then those who, under pretense of explaining nature, sow in the hearts of men the most dispiriting doctrines, whose skepticism is far more affirmative and dogmatical than the decided tone of their adversaries. Under pretense of being themselves the only people enlightened, they imperiously subject us to their magisterial decisions, and would fain palm upon us for the true causes of things the unintelligible systems they have erected in their own heads; while they overturn, destroy, and trample under foot all that mankind reveres, snatch from the afflicted the only comfort left them in their misery; from the rich and great the only curb that can restrain their passions; tear from the heart all remorse of vice, all hopes of virtue, and still boast themselves the benefactors of mankind. 'Truth,' they say, 'is never hurtful to man.' I believe that as well as they, and the same, in my opinion, is a proof that what they teach is not the truth."

* See Leland and Gregory.

Parker's philosophy of God, the effort is ridiculous as it is futile. The wandering mind feels the need of something positive in religion; and having rejected revealed truth, it seeks to attain from reason such baseless dogmas as the rationalist's "idea, sense, and conception of God." The mind of man was made to rest in faith; and when skepticism deprives men of this support, the soul feels more of unrest and deprivation than do the heathen, who rest in a false faith. Unaided reason can doubt, but it can not affirm any thing in relation to God and the future that will satisfy the soul.

Man was not made to be the victim of skepticism. Heathenism is better than this, just as ignorance is better than aberration. Revelation was made for man; made to elevate the races progressively, from a state of nature to a state of grace; made to spread from families to nations, and finally to reach all mankind.

But leaving strictures on doubt and negation, which are to positive religion as night is to the day, let us look at some thoughts which may prepare us more intelligently to consider the positive side of the argument, which maintains that the Christian

Scriptures are a revelation from God, containing the ultimate rule of faith and duty.

All things are progressive in their development. Individually or socially considered, in the life-history of things there is infancy, youth, and maturity. "First the blade, then the ear, then the full corn in the ear." The Scriptures affirm this principle. The family of man are subject to this law. There are ages of infancy, of youth and of maturity. The first law would be one relating to animal wants, and adapted to the period of childhood. Hence the law, "Thou shalt not eat forbidden fruit," as there were no neighbors, and no experience; consequently this was the only adapted law.

The second dispensation would be adapted to man's tuition in the next stage of development. Hence the Mosaic: which, as pictures in a child's primmer, with explanations attached; and a written moral law in the briefest form, gave to a man a more perfect idea of God and of moral duties.

The third stage would be the ultimate and perfect, "the full corn in the ear."

The first stage, or patriarchal, would develop itself from the family into a nation; the second from the nation to all nations. And in this last the law of progress is fulfilled.

Men of the Christian age, together with the knowledge of their own dispensation, get the knowledge generated and transmitted by the two preceding ones. The foundation-principles of these were developed into the final and perfect form of Christianity.

The vital importance of the family, especially its law of duty and obedience, is developed fully in the first dispensation. Abraham is chosen because he will instruct and command his children, Gen. 18: 19. In all ages of revelation, this important principle needed to be understood. Families trained to obey righteous authority, and having their consciences and hearts nurtured by the admonition and fear of God, are the anchor-hope of a free state. Family government and instruction that make intelligent, conscientious, and obedient children, can alone make men fit for citizenship in a Republic. Old and impudent superstitions adverse to Christian education, will have to be overcome before liberty and equality can be established on the basis of enlightened conscience.

Man needs to know also the relation of a state, as a whole, to the divine government; that every state has its probation; that departure from righteous principle will, in the end, bring dissolution and disaster. This is the teaching of the national history of Israel. It exhibits to all ages the principles upon which God administers His government over favored nations, and the discipline which they must incur for national offences against justice and mercy.

These three stages of development are likewise exhibited in the moral progress of individuals. There is first the natural, when animal appetite governs. Second, the intellectual period of growth, when law and penalty govern. Third, for those who rise to it, a dispensation of love and fruit-bearing, when faith governs.

There are likewise the lineaments of these three stages in the advance of each individual that enters the kingdom of heaven on earth. An illustration is furnished in the experience of Paul. Before he became a Jew spiritually, i. e., before he apprehended the law as being from God, and obligatory upon his mind, he was free from a sense of sin; he was sensual, governed by his own natural impulses. Second, when he realized the spirituality of the law, he became a true Pharisee; felt condemned for sin; and endeavored to escape condemnation by works of law. Third, he was made free by faith; and that which before was a work of the intellect and will, without inward love and impulse, now became easy and holy, being prompted by love which was produced by faith in Christ. Through this process, in some degree, passes every individual who rises from nature through conviction into grace.

Hence also the three developments of the name of Jehovah. Al-Shaddai, God of nature or power. Second, Jehovah. A development of the same name known to the fathers, Ex. 6; 3; but, in the second dispensation, to be changed from Al-Shaddai to Jehovah, who now developed himself in moral law and tuition. In the third, Father, Son, and Holy Spirit, the God of power, and developed by law and tuition into the God of grace. Thus by the progressive development of the divine character, has the human mind been raised by faith in that character through the first and second, into the third and ultimate state of knowledge.

With these preliminary remarks, I invite your attention to the following train of thought, as proof of the Necessity of a Written Revelation.

I have in other volumes discussed the details of the statements which follow. An outline view will indicate the course of thought which you will there find more fully and carefully stated. Please notice the form and force of the principles separately, and then in their relation to each other we shall see the necessity of a written revelation, given by divine authority.

Every species of nature may be cultivated. Its properties or faculties may be improved. This is true in a general sense; and especially true as we rise toward the higher species. But the improvement of any species must come from one higher than itself. There may be choice individuals produced by chance circumstances, but no species can raise itself above its natural level.

Now, a distingishing characteristic of man is, that he is both a cultivable and a cultivating being. He cultivates the species of nature below him and fits them to his use, while he himself is capable of moral culture.

But as it requires man's superior powers of intellect and example to cultivate the orders below him, and to raise them above their natural condition, so it requires the powers of a being above man to elevate him, as a moral being, into a new sphere of thought and feeling. The conclusion, therefore, arises not only from the analogy but from the necesity of things, that as man, a higher species, cultivates nature, so Christ from above cultivates man. Let us accept the principle which can not be controverted that no species can raise itself above its natural level without the tuition of a higher mind.

But what are the means of culture adapted to man's nature as a moral being? There are these four, namely, written language, faith, conscience, and example. Faith and conscience are subjective susceptibilities, and written language and example are objective means answering to them; and by the interaction of these, man may be cultivated into the sphere of a superior species. But the external means must be exercised by an agency superior to himself, or he will never rise above his natural selfish and earthly nature.

Notice the facts and their application. Written, or sign-language, is generally supposed to be a natural product of the human reason. However this may be, it is certain that men, after they have attained a settled social condition, always form for themselves a language of signs.

Without this they can not ascend from the first stages of barbarism. Fixed signs of thought are necessary before there can be commercial progress, forms of law, or fixed moral principles.

Sign-language is one of the distinguishing characteristics of the human species. Animals below man can communicate to each other certain ideas, but they can not impress them upon external objects, and thus transmit to others a fixed sign of their thought.

If, then, sign-language is a characteristic of man, and if he can not be elevated from barbarism to social and civil position without it, it would be absurd to suppose that his moral culture can be accomplished without this necessary medium.

Hence, so soon as the primitive nations became settled, and so soon as sign-languages were matured, God gave to man, a brief written record of the past, of his own character, and of his will; and these, together with new and progressive spiritual ideas generated by forms and external types, were rendered permanent in sign-language, and transmitted to the future by the ritual dispensation of Moses.

The second characteristic which distinguishes

man from irrational beings, is faith. Animals receive their knowledge through the senses; man receives most of his knowledge by credence.* All the experience of the past is given to him by faith in testimony. It is faith alone that connects man with the past and the future, with God and the spiritual world. Now, faith depends on written language to reach the past, and on hope to reach the future, and on written revelation to know God. Man is a believing being by nature; and without faith he is no better than the brute, with a perverted faith he is worse.

Faith is the spiritual sense. By it spiritual objects become subjective in the soul, as external physical objects become subjective by sense. By faith in revealed truth, the character of God becomes a conscious influence in the soul. "Faith works by love." "He that loveth, knoweth God, for God is love." Thus by faith the character

* There is a class of philosophers who contend that they receive all their knowledge through the senses. By this method men are allied to animal natures; but the distinguishing characteristic between men and animals is that one receives all his knowledge by sense, the other by sense and above this by faith in testimony. The faculty of credence gives men knowledge of the unknown and the spiritual, which alone distinguishes him from brute natures.

of God, and the life and precepts of God recorded in divine revelation, become united in the moral culture of man. In this way the subjective susceptibility of faith is met by the objective facts of divine revelation.

Mark, now, that without divine truth externally revealed, the susceptibility of faith is injurious and evil to man. Faith controls man's character and his life. If I believe my neighbor to be a bad man, I will feel as though he were so. If a Catholic who has been deprived of the Bible, believes he ought to confess to the Virgin Mary, his conscience will reprove him if he does not do so. Faith forms man's character and his conscience in accordance with what the man believes, whether that be true or false. Faith of itself is blind; it needs a guide as much as a blind man needs eyes. Without revealed religion as the guide of faith, "the blind lead the blind, and both fall into the ditch." Now notice in connection.

Faith is connected with conscience as well as with sign-language in the moral development of man. This brings us to the third fact in the means of human culture. There are two elements in efficient faith, one the external fact, the other the divine authority of the fact. Conscience will respond to no truth unless faith delivers it as coming from God. Great souls, such as Plato, Seneca, and Tully, have spoken great truths; but who cared for these? None but those who did not need them. These were men like others, liable to mistakes, and could give only their opinions, hence they had no authority over men. Their sayings, therefore, could neither awaken or guide the conscience.

God has so constituted the soul, that conscience will enforce no truth upon the life with efficiency, unless it has God in it. The moment faith sees God in truth, that moment conscience awakes and enforces it as a duty. Jesus Christ himself did not teach that his truth would have full reformatory efficacy until after his resurrection. He taught that by his resurrection and the advent of the Spirit, the evidence of divine authority would be given to his truth, and then it would attain new power and application in the souls of men. Truth alone has no power with the conscience. When truth comes in the name of God, then only conscience awakes and enforces obedience.

But mark, now. Conscience, like faith, is

blind without a guide, and with a blind guide it is doubly blind. If a man believe in no God, he will have no conscience in relation to any religious duty. If he believe his god sanctions theft, as do the devotees of Kale, he will steal. If he believe his god sanctions child-sacrifice, conscience will enforce the murder, even against the parental instinct. So faith governs conscience, and both are false and foul without truth. With truth recognized as being only of human origin, faith is dead and conscience inefficient. Hence, the truth, and not only the truth, but God-revealed truth, the truth of God in written language, is the only true guide of the soul.

But if God has so constituted the soul that a written revelation is required in order to moral progress: as God is true, that revelation would be given. As God is true, that revelation has been given in the Christian Scriptures, because the Scriptures are a revelation of truth in progressive dispensations, up to the perfect in love, in precept, and in example.

We come now to the fourth requisite in order to the moral culture of man, a perfect example of human duty, after human duty is revealed.

Instruction is never perfect without example. Oliver Evans could not give his perfect theory of a steam-mill, and say to any one who understood his words and his plan, "Go and build a mill." His common-sense would teach him that the practice has to be learned as well as the theory. The master-workman must take the saw and hatchet, and practice the theory in the presence of the pupil, and put the learner through the routine of the labor. So in all things: theory is only a part of knowledge; the practice has to be learned by effort and example. So in religion. We needed not only the precept, but the example how to practice under the precept in our circumstances. This Christ has given. In the New Testament, Jesus is seen practicing the divine precept, and saying to his disciples, "Follow me."

Again, example is needed not only of moral duty, but of the spirit in which duty is to be discharged. This also is given in the New Testament.

Again, as precepts must be general in their nature, there are many specific applications of them which men could not know were it not for the example of Christ. When a son knows the character, and spirit, and motives of his father, he will be able to judge, in his absence, what his father would do in specific cases, and hence what he would have him to do. So the example and spirit of Christ is a sure guide to his disciples in applying his precepts to the specific duties of life. When the believing mind inquires, what would Christ have me do in this case? the life and Spirit of Jesus, revealed in the Scriptures, will guide to the right conclusion.

But, finally, and above all, in order to man's continued progress toward the perfect, he needs an example that is ever above him, the example of one whose excellence will show him his defects, and whose love and proffered aid will invite him to higher attainments. Faith in Christ's example induces a sense of unworthiness, at the same time that faith in his sacrifice for us, moves the soul by love, and induces self-denial for others. This is the true Christian consciousness, and highest moral condition. Matt. 11: 28–30.

No one will doubt but that a sense of present imperfection and a struggle for higher attainment in holiness, other things being given, is the sure method of moral progress. Now, at the entrance of the straight gate that leads to life stands the Saviour of men. He is ever before his disciples. The light of his perfect character shows them their defects. The love of his heart strengthens and encourages by the way. The mark of the prize of their high calling is to attain the perfection of his character; and to those who are running the race with whatever of knowledge and strength they possess, the divine favor and the divine providence are a conscious blessing and constant guide.

Thus, I think it is plain that the Bible was made for man; that it possesses the characteristics which are alone adapted to develop his moral faculties up to the perfect. A revealed, written revelation is a necessity of man's moral nature. The Bible meets the necessity, and therefore the Bible is of God.

CHAPTER XIII.

REVELATION THE MOTIVE-POWER IN HUMAN PROGRESS.

Has the Bible given impulse and direction in every successful effort that has ever been made for the moral progress of mankind? Let us pass at once to the main and ultimate question as to the facts.

The Bible itself, as every thinking man knows claims that its mission is to enlighten the world, and to advance the moral interests of the human family. It has been shown, as we think, that human nature is so constituted, that revealed religion is necessary in order to the moral development of our race. Do historical facts verify this conclusion?

We have said that the Bible claims to be both light and power in the moral progress of the world. It is however sometimes said that the orthodox party claims more for the Bible than it claims for itself. This may be true when some eulogists of revelation claim for it extraordinary excellences of style, and other extrinsic matters of that sort. But it is not true in regard to the claim of moral light and power. The Bible does claim these, and all friends of revelation should claim them for it. Notice this.

The Old Testament writers speak of their own dispensation as the light of their age; and the minds of the old prophets glow with inspiration when they refer to the increased light and purity of Messiah's age, an age when "the light of the moon was to be as the light of the sun, and the sun itself would shine with sevenfold effulgence." "To the people that sat in darkness and in the valley and the shadow of death," they declared that a "light would spring up." About the last utterance of the last of the prophets refers to the purifying power of the Messiah's dispensation, and to the spiritual light which would be revealed in his day. Mal. 3: 1, 2. "Behold I will send my messenger before me, [John Baptist,] and he shall prepare the way before me; and the Lord, [Messiah,] whom ye seek shall suddenly come to his temple; even the messenger of the covenant whom ye delight in: behold! he shall come, saith the Lord of hosts! But who may abide the day of his coming? and who shall stand when he appeareth? For he shall be like a refiner's fire and like fuller's soap; and he shall sit as a refiner and purifier of silver." That is, the Messiah's dispensation would purify and elevate those who were subjects of its influence. And, ch. 4: 2, 3, while the wicked would be condemned and destroyed, "to those who feared the Lord, the Sun of righteousness would arise with healing in his beams."

To this light of the old dispensation the people who first heard the gospel, and who lived in the transition period, from the death of Christ to the fall of Jerusalem, were exhorted to take heed. Although it shone in a darker dispensation, yet it was a "lamp" in the path that led to a clearer manifestation of divine love and truth. This view of the relations of the Old and New Testament light the Apostle Peter beautifully expresses in his second letter, ch. 1: 19, "We have also a more sure word of prophecy, whereunto ye do well that ye take heed, as unto a light that shineth in a dark place, [age,] until the day dawn, and the day-star, [of the gospel dispensation,] arise in your hearts." The Old Testament dispensation, as interpreted by the inspired prophets, was as a light in the night. The New Dispensation was daylight, which was then dawning in the hearts of believers. They were to take heed to the one till the other was inaugurated.

John Baptist, the forerunner of Jesus, who came to reprove his nation and to call them to repentance, as the proper preparation for the reign of Messiah, was called "a burning and a shining light." The first prophetic announcement of the character of Jesus, after his advent, by the pious Simeon, was that he should be "a light to enlighten the Gentiles, and the glory of his people Israel," and that he would "be set for the fall, [by repentance,] and rising again, [to a higher moral state,] of many in Israel." That is, the Gentile nations should be enlightened by Christ, and "many" of the Jewish nation would feel condemned in the light of his dispensation, and would rise again into the higher moral condition which it required.

John, although himself called a light, affirmed that he was not that light which was to raise a portion of the Jewish people, and enlighten the Gentile nations. "He was not that light, but was sent to bear witness of that light;" "that was the true light that enlighteneth every man that cometh into the world," both Jew and Gentile.

Jesus himself claimed to be "the light of the world." "I am," said he, "come a light into the world, that whosoever believeth in me should not abide in darkness." "I am the light of the world; he that followeth me shall not walk in darkness, but shall have the light of life." The truth which he declared as the basis of condemnation was, that "light had come into the world, and men loved the darkness rather than the light, because their deeds were evil."

The apostles apprehended distinctly that the increased light of revelation was the reforming and the elevating power of the nations. They not only understood the fact, that revelation was the moral life and light of men, but they understood the relations of this fact, and its place in the moral progress of the world. "The darkness," said they, "is past, and the true light now shineth." They speak of the church of Christ as "the light of the world," and Christians as "the Children of the Light." There is, probably, no other topic which suggests illustrations to the minds of the sacred writers more varied and beautiful than this one; and there is none other which conveys to us truth of more vital importance. There is, in my opinion, no figures in human language more striking than those which the inspired writers use in presenting truth under the symbol of light, not only in the past and present, but in the apocalyptic visions of the future. What can be more striking than the figures of the Revelator. Forecasting the period of the Reformation, he speaks of the "two witnesses," the Old and New Testaments, which, clothed in sackcloth, were lying without vitality in the streets; these are elevated into the heavens, from which position they attract the attention of men, and send the rays of the Reformation down into their hearts. The church of Christ, witnessing for truth, is spoken of as "A woman, clothed with the sun, and the moon under her feet, and upon her head a crown of twelve stars."

But I need not dwell upon the fact that the

Scriptures do claim that the truth of revelation is the moral light of the world. There is another fact connected with this subject; one which the cursory reader overlooks, but it is one which relates to the vital power of truth; the Scriptures claim that there is spirit and life in the truth which they reveal. To this life of the light, I ask your attention, before the historical analysis which is to follow. It is well to ascertain accurately the apostolic conception, and the breadth of the Scripture claim, before an appeal to external testimony.

To see an evil is one thing; to lead men to feel the turpitude of evil, in itself, in themselves and in the sight of God, is quite another thing. We have already noticed this fact. It will not be necessary to dwell on it here. Suffice it to say, that in order to the moral progress of men two things are necessary. First, that men should see the evil; and second, that they should feel such a sense of the evil as will lead them to turn from it, and seek a higher life. Light is necessary to see the evil. A sense of God and duty with that light, is necessary to lead men from the evils which the light reveals.

Now, this reproving or convicting power accompanies the light of revealed religion. There may be intellectual culture where there is no moral purity. The first benefit is scarcely a blessing without the last. A knowledge of right and duty only renders one a greater hypocrite unless he have moral sense and moral life sufficient to conform to his own convictions. Now, this reproving power, which leads men to feel the evil of sins which they perceive, the Scriptures claim for themselves as a spiritual efficacy which accompanies revealed truth. Let us notice and illustrate this fact.

We have shown elsewhere that truth has power over the moral nature of men, only so far as a sense of God and duty is in it. There needs to be life as well as light in that truth which has reforming power in the world. This life-power the sacred writers claim as belonging to the gospel. It is a power by which men feel reproved or condemned for the sins which truth reveals to them, a power which leads them to disapprove evils in themselves and others "made manifest by the light."

Christ is spoken of as being not only the "light," but the "life" of men. The second Adam gave not only light to the intellect, but life to the heart. He was a "life-giving" as well as a "light-giving" Spirit. "The words that I speak unto you," said Jesus, "they are spirit and they are life." "I am the light of the world. He that followeth me shall not walk in darkness, but shall have the light of life." "I am the way, the truth, and the life." Now, this life, or reproving, or convicting power, is the glory of the gospel. Without this, the intellect may be enlightened, while the conscience will be dead and the heart corrupt. Hence Jesus said, "Ye will not come unto me lest your deeds should be reproved." The one thing needful, after the understanding is enlightened in relation to moral duties, is this reproving life in the conscience of men, which produces "repentance unto life." The Holy Ghost, which gave the God-sense to truth, is this reproving power. The divine Spirit gives life to the soul, by the truth. Christ taught that when the Comforter, which is the Holy Ghost, should come into the world, He would persuade, or reprove, the world of sin, righteousness and judgment.

The disciples understood that without this moral power, the mere intellectual light of truth would increase sin instead of producing holiness. Hence they said, "Christ hath made us ministers of the New Testament; not of the letter, but of the spirit; for the letter killeth, but the spirit giveth life." Paul, in his letter to the Christians at Ephesus, states with great distinctness the effect and the necessity of gospel truth, both as an enlightening and reproving power. 5: 13, "All things that are reproved are made manifest by the light; for whatsoever doth make manifest is light: wherefore [the gospel saith] Awake, thou that sleepest, and arise from the dead, and Christ shall give thee light." That is, the light of revealed religion shows the moral evils which exist in the heart and in the world; and the life-power of the Spirit accompanying that light, leads us to feel the guilt of these evils.

Notice, now, an instance of the influence and practical operation of this moral power of truth, as it affected the reformation of the world in the apostolic age. The same principle we shall see is applicable in all other cases, and in all time.

Take the case of the city of Ephesus, to the Christian inhabitants of which Paul writes the passage we have quoted. The apostle describes this city as sitting in darkness, and her citizens as corrupted by the practice of the most debasing vices. He says to the Christians, "Ye were sometime darkness, but now are ye light in the Lord. Walk as children of the light, and have no fellowship with the unfruitful works of darkness, but rather reprove them; for it is a shame even to speak of those things which are done of them in secret." Such was the celebrated city of Ephesus when the light and reproving power of the gospel reached her. What was necessary in her case?

Intellectual light was not what the men of Ephesus wanted. They lived in the Augustan age, the noon-day of ancient civilization. They lived when the light of reason had reached its meridian in the ancient world. They lived in the Eclectic age, when the best thoughts were collected from Plato and all the great thinkers that had gone before. It was the age of Seneca and Pliny, of Tacitus, Josephus, and Plutarch, the crowning authors of the ancient literature, in morals, history, science, and religion.

And this city of Ephesus was one of the points in Asia where art and letters had done all they could do for human culture. Diana of the

Ephesians was one of the purest shrines at which the old world worshiped; and her temple was one of the most magnificent structures that was ever erected and adorned by human hands.—About the time that Paul wrote the passage which we have quoted, describing the appalling corruption which prevailed in the city, Pliny, one of the wisest and most refined men of his age, speaks of Ephesus as "one of the luminaries of Asia." The one considered her as full of light, the other looked upon her as full of darkness. Both views were true, according to the standard by which the writers formed their judgment. Pliny saw her as the seat of the best civilization and the highest culture that a people without revelation had ever attained. But underneath the glare of vain-glory, Paul saw a degree of corruption that defiled her very heart. She was "a whited sepulcher, full of dead men's bones." The light that was in her was darkness. Those who lived in it said, "Behold, we see!" and the baptism of their sacred rites, by which they sought to purify themselves, only infected them with baser pollution.

What was needed, now, in order to reform and save this people? Was it civilization?

This they had attained in the highest degree which unaided reason could achieve. Was it philosophy? Some of the most celebrated schools were in this city. Was it perfection of art? The best models of the age, some of which still exist as artistic wonders for the moderns, were at Ephesus; and it is recorded that the personal accomplishments and taste of her citizens were celebrated throughout surrounding regions. All these she had, as many cities of modern Europe have still, and yet, having eyes, her citizens saw not the prevailing corruption; and having ears, they heard not the sentence of condemnation written against them.

What they needed, first of all, was light to discern the evil nature of sin; and second, that personal sense of the evil which would lead them to escape from it, and endeavor to rescue others. Until they saw their sin and felt its evil, they could make no advances in moral character.

Now, Paul affirmed in relation to these men, and to this subject, two things—that whatever they saw to be evil in their former practice was made manifest to them by the moral light of the gospel, and that whatsoever makes sin manifest, as the gospel does, is light.

Once more. Notice that this state of intellectual culture and moral blindness was not confined to the old world. The same is true of the moderns; although our own country does not remind one of the union between culture and sin, as do the cities of Europe. The art and intellectual culture of Europe is the culture of the few as against the many. Paris, with her academy, her columns, her galleries of painting, her statuary, her cathedrals, her philosphers, her oratorios, her taste and fashion, her every thing that is deemed a mark of high intellectual culture, Paris, with all these, is the brothel of nations, a city where every species of moral corruption festers and infects the inhabitants, and spreads moral contagion over the continent.

I have stood in her galleries at Versailles and the Louvre, and felt in my soul that her models of art were a curse to the people. They are adapted to gild the memory of those who, being corrupt in heart and profligate in practice, are now suffering the hell that awaits selfish and impure minds. Their undraped statuary imparts the infection of the old world's guilt to the new. The pictures of the old masters, and from them down even to David, sanctify the deeds of devils under the name of kings and cardinals. Thus the popular mind is led by art to reverence despots and evil-doers. Their religion is almost as corrupt as the orgies of Ephesus, and their moral corruption similar to hers. In my opinion, while art might lose something, progress and morality would gain much, if the next outbreak in Paris should destroy all the Papist oratorios and all the public galleries in the city. What is true of Paris, is true likewise of all the great cities of the continent where the people are without the light of revelation. Culture and crime prevail together, to some extent, even in Protestant cities; but there is as much moral difference between the Protestant cities of Philadelphia, Geneva and Aberdeen on the one hand, and Rome, Naples, and New Orleans on the other, as there is between daylight and darkness.

Intellectual culture without Christian culture, is a painted harlot, who lives in the night; and, decorated in the tinsel of art and letters, allures the weak and the wicked to hell. Were there no hope for mankind but that which art, letters, and intellectual culture produces, despotism and skepticism would reign over the earth, and the hope of moral progress, of human freedom, and human happiness, might be abandoned forever. Men might be as cultivated as was Robespierre, and yet become as dark-minded and as desperate as he. They might be as polished externally as was Webster the murderer of Dr. Parkman, while yet internally they might be as wicked as he. John Newton had the same mind and the same intellectual culture when engaged in the slave-trade, and in low and vicious practices that he afterward possessed when his muse charmed and elevated the hearts of all those who listened to him.

In many and striking forms Christ taught men the difference between intellectual and Christian culture. The one without the other is "the whited sepulcher," "the hidden grave," the darkness or "night" of the soul. The one pertains to man's moral nature, his affections and his conscience, the other to his intelligence. The one without the other engenders selfishness and hypocrisy; but intellectual culture, used and sanctified by a living conscience and pure affections, secures all human good to its possessor, and leads him to labor for the good of the world. When the intellect moves to the work of human elevation, the power which gives the impulse and secures permanency, is generated in the heart and conscience. Men with intellectual light alone may make advances without moral principles, as they have done often in France, South America, and elsewhere; but without moral principle, which gospel faith produces, permanent progress is impossible.

With these principles and discriminations in mind, notice some other evidences of the fact that all human progress, both ancient and modern, has its origin in the truth and power of revealed religion; and that without this, the hope of reform is fallacious, and if progress were attained, it could not be permanent.

It is a historical fact which has not been sufficiently noticed, that human nature is always below revelation. This fact indicates the divine origin of revelation. Great discoveries are usually the product of preceding ages of thought. One mind in the end develops the idea; but it is the fruitage of the age ripened in that particular mind. A pearl is found; but the location had been indicated by previous researches. But revealed religion is something different from this.

It is separate from and superior to the thought of the age. It calls the wisdom of the world foolishness, and introduces a new stand-point and starting-point, around which it gathers what was valuable in the old, and destroys the remainder. Hence it will always be found true that a struggle is necessary to bring up the human mind and keep it up to the level of revealed religion, and that revealed religion produces that struggle. The human mind naturally falls below it; hence frequent struggles are necessary to restore it from its relapses. Even those who profess to be the friends of the dispensation, retrograde so soon as its power is in any wise abated; and new applications of the same power have to be made to rescue them, and bring them up again nearer to the requirements of their dispensation.

No one will doubt but that the theology of Moses was antagonistic to that of Egypt, and to that of all the nations with which the Israelites had intercourse. Its great aim was to destroy idolatry, to remove physical and moral impurities, and establish the worship of one true God, Jehovah. But the Jews, although all their traditions were in favor of monotheism, and all their experiences such as were adapted to drive them from idolatry, were constantly falling into the vices and idolatries of surrounding nations. Their history is a record of sad departures from the purity of the Mosaic economy.

Now, the question is, by what means was the advanced system maintained and reformation produced, when the people had again dropped down to their natural level? We answer, by the power of revealed truth, and by this alone. "Whatsoever was reproved in Israel, was made manifest by the light," and "whatsoever does make manifest is light."

Their defections from Monotheism were shown to them by referring them to the light of the law of Moses. This alone could show them the evil of polytheism, for no other system existed in the world that did not favor the evil. The evil being revealed by the law, they were reproved out of the same law for departing from its requirements, and in this way alone reformations were produced. The instances of reformation by the light and power of the revealed religion I need not to enumerate. The relapses were all recovered, and the nation finally delivered from all disposition to idolatry, by the Bible, and by the providence of God working in harmony with the dispensation, punishing departures and encouraging reform.

When the nation was almost lost in the surrounding darkness, the Reformation under Josiah was produced by the law alone. "The Book" found, as Luther found it afterwards in the convent, was the light and power of the rescue.

In the later periods of the dispensation, the old prophets stood up in the solemn grandeur of their mission, to reprove the rulers and the people, and restore them to obedience to the law. The voices of Jeremiah, of Isaiah and Ezekiel, are heard in tones of sorrow, instruction, and reproof, reverberating through the nation. They held aloft the law, and showed to the people that the judgments of God would come, or had come, upon them for departing from it. They gave the law a spiritual and practical import, a charactistic of the true preacher; they enforced it by the authority of God; and spoke almost with the tongue of an evangelist of a future Messiah. Thus, in the light of the law they reproved in the name of God: and if reformation was not produced, they led the people to feel that judgment came upon them for disobedience; and thus their captivities and sufferings tended finally to cure their errors.

Now, I need not say that by this process, and this alone, was the worship of one God at length established in the world. By the law of Moses, and the administration of reproof by the prophets, the thing was accomplished, and in no other way. Thus the law was a schoolmaster to bring us to Christ. When the evil of idolatry was cured, and ideas of the Messiah created by the Mosaic ritual, the world was prepared for a higher dispensation.

One other topic here is worthy of notice. It is a part of the history of monotheism that has not been sufficiently studied. I allude to the history of the Arabians, as it connects itself with the Old Testament on the one side, and with Islamism on the other. The Arabs claim Abraham, the first reformer of the world, as their father. Ishmael was the son of the father of the faithful; but his son by a foreign wife; yet to Ishmael also was the promise given, that he should inherit, but in an inferior degree, the blessing of Abraham. Other descendants of Abraham were mingled in Idumea, constituting two lines of the Abrahamic family, the Arabic and the Jewish. They have the same relation to the true religion that the two sons have to

Abraham, or Esau and Jacob to Isaac. Through the true son comes the true gospel; the other is a degree removed from it. But the fact is, that both lines recognize and worship the same one God: from both originate the reformers of idolatry. The Arabs are now, in this respect, about where the Jews were before the coming of Christ. They, like the Jews, have frequently relapsed into the idolatry and vices of surrounding nations; yet before Mohammed there were many reformers who restored monotheism in some of the tribes. But the points at which this history connects itself with our subject are, first, the Mohammedans are monotheists; second, they worship Jehovah, the God of Abraham and Moses; third, mark it, this reformation of the Arabian tribes, which restored the worship of of the one God, was effected by Mohammed through the light and power of the patriarchal and Mosaic dispensations. The truth which the prophet uses to kill idolatry is drawn from the history of Abraham and the precepts of Moses. The 14th chapter of the Koran is entitled "Abraham." The patriarch is introduced as praying for the suppression of idolatry—"Keep me and my children from the worship of idols;

they have seduced part of the people." The authority of Moses is likewise recognized, and he is frequently introduced as denouncing idolatry and commanding the worship of Jehovah.

Thus, the evidence is palpable and incontrovertible, that the worship of one God revealed in the Old Testament Scriptures, has been the reforming power of the whole world, so far as man is rescued from idolatry. The two branches of the Abrahamic family have done the work. Mohammedans are now, in this one respect, where the Jews were before Christ, and where the unbelieving Jews are still. All that they have in advance of heathen polytheism is by the revealed religion of the Old Testament, and the authority of Jehovah as therein revealed. All that we have in advance of them starts from this point. This brings us to the gospel dispensation, the "true light that now shineth."

The prophets of the old dispensation, as we have noticed, had foretold the sevenfold light of the Messianic age. The last prophetic utterance Mal. 3: 1–4, announces that Christ would send his messenger, John Baptist, before him; that he would suddenly come in his temple; but that his dispensation would be "as a refiner's fire," a moral power, purifying the world and the church.

John Baptist came, and affirming that the kingdom of heaven was at hand, he called the nation to repentance; thus practically promulgating the truth that reformation was necessary in order to enter the Messiah's kingdom. This was the burden of his baptism, "The axe is laid at the root of the tree." The separating fan is in the hand of the Messiah. He will separate the chaff from the wheat, gather the wheat into his garner, and burn the chaff with unquenchable fire.

Jesus came, preaching reformation and a higher life. He denounced the traditions of the Jewish teachers. He selected men without literary or philosophical attainment. He imbued them with a new spirit, and with power from on high; and commissioned them to revolutionize all forms of power in church and state; promising divine aid and supervision until the work should be accomplished.

You know the result. You know the struggle and the success of the truth in the apostolic age. As it was in Ephesus, so it was in other cities. When Jesus died, the old world had its greatest intellectual light, and its greatest moral darkness. The truth and power of the gospel was a purifying element, reforming and elevating out of the mass of corruption a large company of the men and women of that age.

In establishing a new system, with new powers and principles, the agency of the Divine Author must be interposed, of course; just as every new geological advance requires divine interposition. But as human nature is always be low the revealed religion which is designed to reform and elevate it, the corrupt age, and the dark ages which followed, were a natural sequence. The last of the apostles was not in his grave, and the visible power which established the New Testament had scarcely subsided, before humanity lapsed into error. To the light of the apostolic age there succeeded clouds, darkened by depravity and tinged by superstition. When earthly power could not subdue the church, it allied itself with her, and thus corrupted her truth. This adulterous union of church and state is the great dragon on the Continent, and the little dragon in England, Rev. 12, et seq., and from the period of the adulterous union between church and state the light of truth waned into the total eclipse of the dark ages—ages without a Bible.

But out of the darkness a light sprung up which has shone more and more down to our day. Now, our last inquiry is, has revealed religion been the source and the power of reformation and moral progress in the world, under the Christian dispensation, and from the dark ages until now?

We need not inquire concerning the causes which immediately introduced the dark ages. Suffice it to say, that during the period from the sixth to the fifteenth century, the light of revelation was vailed. The Scriptures were no longer in the vernacular tongue of the people. Both church and state were without a Bible. The dawn of reformation begins with Wickliffe and Huss. Their translations and preaching antedate the art of printing, and the other great inventions of the fifteenth century. The art of printing no doubt greatly aided the Reformation; but printing has in itself no reformatory moral power. Whether it advances or retards the civil and moral progress of men, depends on the things printed. The enemies of the Reformation used the press as freely as the reformers. The press infected the continent with atheism in the days of Voltaire, and the press strengthened the power of despotism under Robespierre. The press can do no more than disseminate the thought of the age, whether that be bad or good. Truth is stronger than error; hence the press is an auxiliary in the world's enlightenment. But light without moral principle has no real reformatory power. It does not create conscience, and hence wants the element of permanent moral progress.

Luther is identified as the man of the Reformation. Whence did Luther draw his power? A benighted monk, he found a copy of the Bible in the convent of Erfurth, as Josiah did in the temple of old. The Bible enlightened Luther. He translated it into the vernacular tongue of his country, and it enlightened the people. Every shaft that the reformers hurled at the Papal demon was drawn from the Bible. Nine tenths of the literature of the Reformation was biblical. That the Bible made the reformers is as true as that the reformers produced the Reformation by the same means. About the facts in the case there can be no controversy. The dark ages were dissipated, and the Reformation accomplished by the light and power of revealed religion.

You have, no doubt, read the recently published history of the Dutch Republic, by Motley. If you have not, get it at once. It will give you the detailed statement of the struggle between the Bible power and the Papal devil in the Netherlands, a struggle, the successful issue of which placed Holland in the forefront of the civilization of the age, furnished an asylum for the persecuted in other nations, and developed a degree of moral progress greatly in advance of the times. That the Bible power achieved this moral victory for humanity, freedom, and religion, can not be questioned.

It is conceded that the basis for the Reformation in England was laid by Tindall's translation. Besides this, during the struggle in the Netherlands, multitudes of the persecuted fled to England, and carried the seeds of Bible truth with them across the Channel. Thus was begun the progress that was rendered permanent by the translation under King James.

Another stage of progress in civil and religious freedom was initiated by the Puritans. To them it is conceded, even by Macaulay, that England owes all that places her in advance of other nations of Europe. To the Puritans, Quakers, and especially to the Baptists we owe all of religious liberty that we possess in America. And yet who dare deny that all these stages of progress were gained by the Bible power? The questions of those ages of progress were Bible questions. The conscience that strengthened true moral heroes to endure and to triumph was Bible-made conscience. The issues between them and their opponents were Bible issues. Luther's moving issue was justification by faith against the Papist error of justification by penance and indulgences. The Dutch and the Scotch fought against the powers of darkness, and triumphed under the same banner. The Puritans inscribed on their banner "Bible faith and practice against forms." The pure Bible was their watchword. Wesley's Reformation was purely religious, but, like preceding advances, it was founded on Bible principle, experience against profession. So the principle of Penn was non-conformity to the world, against a worldly church. But more than all, it was Bible faith which gave strength of heart and conscience and will to all these reformers; so that they braved dangers, suffered persecutions, subdued the wilderness, and achieved all the civil and religious progress which the world possesses.

This historic analysis might be run through all the details of human progress. So far as the human family has advanced in moral culture, with its concomitant blessings of civil liberty and social comfort, that advance has been achieved, even in limited localities, by Bible light and power.

Take an epitome of instances and illustrations. In my school-days we had a map in our geographies which gave us an apprehension of the degree of civilization existing in different countries of the globe. Those regions which were the most advanced in civil and moral culture, were light; the utterly pagan regions were black; those regions partially civilized were partially radiated. Now, upon that map, which I took pains to inquire for and examine very recently, the degree of national enlightenment corresponds precisely with the amount of Bible knowledge prevalent among the people. There is no exception to this. It is universal over the whole earth. The Bible is the light and life of the moral world, just as distinctly as the sun is the light and life of the physical world.

The local illustrations of this fact are striking. I have had the privilege, in various portions of the old and new world, of noticing evidences that have left lasting impressions on my heart.

Various states of Germany contain a mixed population, some Protestant, some Papal inhabitants. Now, just in proportion to the Protestant element does moral progress and civil liberty exist. Take Belgium as the starting-point. Travel up the Rhine and through the German states toward Rome, and the amount of progress can be gaged accurately by the amount of Bible knowledge among the people. As you approach Rome, the seat of Papal power and superstition, the darkness can be felt. There the Bible is totally withheld from the masses, and the despotism of the rulers, and the degradation of the people, and the superstition of the whole, are almost equal to that of Central Asia; while vice and crime are more prevalent than they are in Central Africa.

Pass with me, now, through Scotland and Ireland. Scotland has one curse in common with Ireland, the habit of using ardent spirits prevalent among all classes. But apart from this, the peasantry are equal to any in Europe.

In the cities of Edinburg and Glasgow there is a degree of poverty and vice in some of the poorer streets, as in High and Cowgate streets, Edinburg, which is revolting. I saw nothing like it in Aberdeen. On inquiring of an intelligent gentleman the reasons of the phenomenon, he said most of the mass of depravity accumulated in these pens was made up of Irish Catholics and similar elements; and that scarcely any of it originated with the Bible-reading population of the country.

Pass from Glasgow to Belfast, in Ireland; and from Belfast through Dublin to the south of the island. In this journey, as you leave the Bible-reading north, and pass to the Catholic south, you pass from light and morals into the heart of one of the most degraded and superstitious regions that there is in Europe. Perhaps, after the masses of Rome and Naples, there is none more so in Christendom. The emigration of this ignorant and superstitious population to American cities, brings a curse with it. "Democratic mobs" are often referred to in Europe. The accusers do not know that the mobs are composed of the Catholic masses, from their own country, and that intemperance here is mostly, cause and curse of foreign origin.

Now, let us look a moment, over the different sections of our own country, and it will be seen that the most intelligent and moral population of the world, take them en masse, is in that portion of the Union where the people are most generally instructed in Bible principles, and precepts; while in other sections of our land vice and ignorance prevail just in proportion as the people are deprived of the Bible; or in proportion as they suppress Bible truth in professedly Christian churches. In the one section principles and practices are maintained that would have appalled the men of the same section twenty years ago. In the other, it is hoped the light is advancing.

It is likewise true that all the moral reforms for which our land is distinguished, so far as they have succeeded, have been initiated and advanced by the Bible light and power in the hearts and consciences of reformers. The temperance movement began in the church; and the process of enlightenment was carried forward almost exclusively by Christians. Search the record, and you will find that the impulse and the direction were both given by Bible readers. I know the final appeal has been to legislation; but legislation can do nothing until sufficient light is disseminated and sufficient conscience produced in relation to the evil to be reformed. Our legislation, in some States, has gone in advance of the moral sentiment of the masses, and reaction has ensued; and the reform will never become prevalent until the light and moral power of the Bible produce sufficient conscience to sustain it. There only is the moral principle that creates perseverance, there the benevolence that prompts to persistent self-denial for human good.

So in relation to the anti-slavery reform. In England; the Christian sentiment of the nation began, carried forward, and consummated the work of emancipation. In this country, the first fifteen years were spent entirely in moral endeavor by Bible men. It is true that a large portion of the churches withheld their influence, especially those churches rendered conservative by wealth, or connection with the sin; but after all, it is true that in every region of the free States where the reform was urged perseveringly, and one advance after another secured, in every such instance, it will be found that the Bible power was the impulse, and Christians the agents in the work. Mr. Garrison was a true and praiseworthy reformer, but the claim either that he originated the movement or announced the principle of immediate emancipation is not true. Rev. John Rankin in his letters on Slavery; and before him Rev. Mr. Thomas, of Southern Ohio, had proclaimed, on Scripture principles, the duty of emancipation.

Mr. Garrison, in that spirit which always characterizes the best minds, acknowledged in a convention assembled at Cincinnati, in the presence of Mr. Rankin and the assembled audience, his indebtedness to that gentleman for principle and impulse in the anti-slavery cause; this statement he subsequently inscribed in a volume which he presented to the aged veteran.

The paper published by Mr. Garrison had a very limited circulation, and that mostly among those who needed no conviction of the evil of slavery. Its influence was but little in the country. The West, including New York had anti-slavery societies in all the States, and in many counties and churches. There were, both at the East and West, hundreds of lecturers, and tens of thousands of publications. Mr. Garrison's name was prominent and he was popular with a clique, but he was not an accepted writer with one in one hundred of the anti-slavery men of America. There were parties who claimed to be anti-slavery men, par excellence, of whom this could not be said; but these were self-elated and impracticable parties, united by idiosyncrassies, and utterly infeasible in their aims, as they were uncharitable in their spirit. Their influence in some cases hindered rather than helped the cause of liberty.

But, enough, The idea that human progress can be achieved without the Bible is a fallacy, branded as such both by the principles developed in the preceding chapter, and by the historical statements and illustrations of the present one. The truth of this is verified by the facts of history. Revealed religion is the Alpha and the Omega of human progress.

CHAPTER XIV.

REFORMERS AND THEIR RELATION TO CHRISTIANITY.

We have heretofore had occasion to speak of Reformers, and the value of their labors. We would now present in a more extended form what we believe to be the true value of reform efforts, and their relation to the gospel of Christ. Society, we are sure, can be advanced to its best condition only by Christianity, and reforms can achieve abiding good only through the principles and faith of the gospel. Many reformers seem not to know it, but it is true nevertheless, that the principles of Christianity, give impulse and guidance to every advance in the moral progress of the world.

Seneca and Plato who represent the highest

moral attainment, apart from revealed religion, say nothing about the intrinsic selfishness of living for the good of the individual or class, and not for the good of man, in proportion to his need. They do not announce the principles of fraternity and equality. They do not require those who have means, light, liberty, to make self denials to confer the advantages they possess upon those deprived of them. They did not proclaim as a truth, requiring practical recognition, the Fatherhood of God, and the brotherhood of men. They do not say 'love your enemies,' 'God is love; and he that loveth is born of God.' And yet, these very principles, which are found in the people, and no where else, are the life of all true reforms and without their application the removal of social and moral evils is impossible.

But a knowledge of right principles is not all that is necessary. What the world needs is an increase of benevolence, something that tends to destroy selfishness, and lead one man to labor for another's good. Knowledge of the right is needful, but it is not the one thing needful in removing evil from the world. We want something within, that empowers conscience and actuates the will in accordance with our conviction of right. Mere conviction of right, without love for man, can be bribed, whether within the church or without. Wendell Phillips, if he had been born at the south, might have been the duplicate of Foote of Mississippi. His natural characteristics are more like the ex-senator than like those of any other man in the land. To recognize the principles of reform in the gospel, or even to have them transferred to the intellect, is not all that is needed. Man wants the impulse of the conscience and heart, in connection with the conviction of right.

Now a selfish mind becomes benevolent only by faith in Jesus Christ: a true faith in this divine manifestation of God, awakens all the moral powers of the believer and prompts him to live for the good of man, as did the Redeemer. It imparts not only the purpose, but likewise the power to conform to the accepted principle. Thus the gospel reveals the principles of reform, and imparts the disposition to obedience. There are advocates of right that do not confess the one, nor possess the other. But without vitalizing faith, reform will be a mere struggle of natural benevolence, against the predominating follies and wrongs of society. The struggle will promote self-righteousness in the reformer, and increase malignity in the evil doer. Those who advocate truth without love, may create conscience even in those who resist, and do good in that way; but the sublime, the Christ-like in reform, unites truth and love as motive and means to remove from the world whatever injures man.

All efforts for reform of evils, or for moral progress in the world, brings out men into three relations in connection with the movement. The Conservatives, the Reformers and the Radicals. John Baptist was a Radical, Jesus was a Reformer. The Scribes and Pharisees were Conservatives. Every reform has its John Baptists; men who go before and awaken the people to discussion and action. The Reformers follow the Radicals. The conservatives resist his appeal and his principles. These John Baptists, like their great prototype, are usually born to their vocation. It is in their nature. It is sometimes their religion. In diet and in clothing, against evil habits, and evil usages, as the original Baptizer, they lift up their voice like a trumpet, and summon men to repent and prepare the way for a better future.

Among the radical class, there always have been, and there always will be ultra and unwise men, who do injury by leading those who sympathize with them to extreme and impracticable efforts. Such men arrested the progress of the Lutheran Reformation by urging extreme and disorganizing views of civil and religious doctrine. In efforts to abate the evil of absurd fashions which deform the person, pervert the taste, and destroy health, they often go to the opposite extreme, and lose all proper apprehension of the proprieties of sex, both in regard to clothing and occupation.

In dietetics they do not discriminate between what is proper for an invalid, and what is proper for a person in good health. An arm, the muscles of which had been injured by over-labor, or in any other way, would give constant pain, and be permanently debilitated, by wielding daily a five pound hammer; while the same exercise would not only be salutary, but necessary to the growth and development of a healthy arm. The same principle obtains in regard to the stomach, and all the functions of the human body. The amount, variety, and kind of healthy food, ought to be taken in view of health, labor and climate.

So the Fourier mania, a few years since, came in with its impracticable theories, to arrest the efforts of those who would have aided labor in its struggle against the extortions of capital.

So the Quakers broke their own power, although they were among the best class of Reformers that have ever appeared in the world. They maintained many truths in regard to the Spirit, and against the empty forms of religion, but they marred their movement by opposition to all music, to all variety in dress, and to all amusements.

Thus while extreme conservatism selfishly resists moral progress and spiritual religion, extreme radicalism, often discourages Reformers, who are aiming to accomplish good objects, and deforms the reform they would promote by a wrong spirit and extreme action.

The fact that the conservatives resist or discourage all reforms in the beginning, does not prove that all new things, or all extreme views are either desirable or practicable. But shall philanthropists cease action because others act unwisely? The Christian is called by the voice of God, and the sanctified reason within him, to oppose whatever injures man temporally or spiritually. A father from the very nature of his regard for his son, can not care for him in one respect, and have no regard for him in another. He can not save him from slavery, and yet not desire to save him from intemperance. The Christian, who is like Christ, will endeavor to save man from all evils that injure his body or his soul; and he will labor to promote "the beautiful the true and the good" among men, both in temperance and in spiritual things. Standing then between the extremes of non-action and of ultra action in regard to alleged evils, what is right and wrong in regard to some of the living reform questions of the times?

CHAPTER XV.

WOMAN'S RIGHTS, WOMAN'S SUFFRAGE.

The discussions concerning the position and privileges of woman, should not be ignored, because there are those who, in the name of "woman's rights," seek unwise or impracticable ends.

The parental and marital rights of women should be protected by proper legislation, where such rights are not now fully protected. Wages should be granted to all sexes and ages, in proportion to the value of the service rendered, and to women, in some cases, beyond the service rendered. Opportunity should be granted to all to engage in professions and employments not inconsistent with sex, and the relations of individuals to society. But there are difficulties in adjusting even these proper claims of women;

and there are claims made for women as rights, which, beyond question, would work great wrong if they were achieved.

As in all other cases, the advocates of woman's rights, both wise and unwise, set out with the plea that all reforms are resisted in the beginning; hence a good plea is made a reason with some for urging reform into deformity. Others claim, in the name of advancing civilization, acceptance for schemes that would retard progress, and react upon those who are making wise efforts for the good of women, as the weaker, and hence, in some respects, the worthier division of the race.

The introductory dispensation of Moses, although "it made nothing perfect," recognized, in various ways, the natural and social province of the sexes. Those of one sex who wore the apparel of the other, were declared to be "an abomination unto the Lord." The New Dispensation not only emancipated woman from the imperfect divorce laws to which she was previously subjected, but in spiritual benefits she became the peer of man. "In Christ Jesus there is neither Jew nor Gentile, bond nor free, male nor female." The freedom of association in religious service is attested, not only by the presence of women, but by the voice of women in the devotions of the early churches. But while this freedom and elevation of women is achieved by the Gospel, there is that care which characterizes the work of God, both in nature and grace, that the modesty of nature, and the dependence of the sexes, should not be violated.

Woman is assigned her proper place, both in devotion and service, as in the case of Phœbe, the deaconess; but the propagation of the Gospel and the public service of the churches were exclusively intrusted to men. Jesus sent no women with the Seventy, or with the Twelve, to teach in the synagogues, or preach to the nations. The Apostles ordained no women. No women were endowed by the Spirit to be pastors, teachers, or evangelists. These facts should settle the question on the subjects to which they relate. Some women prophesied, but prophecy evidently was understood to be a special spiritual communication, not a stated, or regular service. Women, well instructed in the truth, taught the younger women at home; and the children and youth of both sexes were instructed by them; but they were inhibited from public disputation, and from teaching in public assemblies.

Women prayed occasionally in the social assemblages of the primitive church; but they were forbidden to pray without being veiled; the veil being the badge of sex in the apostolic age. Badges change, but the principle does not. And women should never disregard the proprieties of sex in the worship of God, who created man male and female. Unity of spirit in worship, does not annul natural laws and proprieties. The utterances of prayer and experience in devotional meetings, by pious women, often do good; but posture, gesture, and declamation in promiscuous assemblies, is uncomely and unscriptural; and while good women engage in the one, natural modesty, and religious meekness, will prompt them to avoid the other.*

It is noticeable, that in the parables of Christ,

* A female writer, who has done much good by a devout life and labor, in order to support a theory that hinders, rather than furthers, her work, has misconstrued the Scriptures in regard to woman's position as a teacher. She argues that the Holy Spirit, upon the day of Pentecost, fell in miraculous tongues upon women, as upon men. Nothing can be more obvious than the fallacy of this teaching. It is not possible for an unbiased mind to read the second chapter of the Acts, and err on this subject. The miracle took place in a public assemblage, probably in a court of the temple, where no women were ever present.

where women are introduced as laborers in connection with Gospel progress, home duties are selected as illustrating their province and their work. One puts leaven in three measures of meal; illustrating the impartation of Gospel instruction and life to the household, by those in charge of a family. Another sweeps the house, until she finds the lost piece of money; that is, she seeks by purity of home life and teaching, the salvation of a child yet unregenerate. The shepherd who has lost a sheep goes abroad to find it. The woman who has lost a piece of money seeks for it in the house. The aim is the same, the province is different. What did Jesus mean by teaching the same thing in two different parables, the only difference being the different provinces of the sexes? Home labor is for woman, public labor is for man.

There are some natural laws and moral principles that may be safely trusted, as a general guide in settling the question of woman's province in the social and political world.

The physical differences in the constitution of the sexes cannot be violated, without injury to the violator, and wrong on the part of those who urge the violation. Woman is physically the weaker sex. Women who labor in the open air, are more robust than those who live mostly in the shade; but they are not nearly so strong as men who engage in the same labor, under the same circumstances. They have not strength to do, or endure, what men can easily accomplish. In some cases the labor would kill the one, that only gives proper development to the other. Hence, in the nature of things, the province of woman's labor must always be different from that of man's labor. When this law is violated, women become coarse, and lose the feminine graces both of form and of mind; while men, by the same labor, attain a robustness that is recognized by both sexes as a proper attribute of manhood. Where men and women thus unite in out-door labor, man is invariably the manager, and woman the passive worker; his mind, therefore, loses no vigor, while hers loses both vigor and vivacity; and her body loses natural grace and motion.

Women can not go to war; nor to the fields to clear the lands, which they sometimes cultivate. They can not build houses, or make railroads or canals, or any other public works. They can have nothing to do with the commerce of any country, by building ships, or sailing them. Nor can they engage in managing the public interests of the land. All these public labors are interdicted to women by the laws of nature and civilization. The fact that some women have engaged in all these employments, argues either an unnatural prepension in such persons, or an evil in the arrangements of society, that renders such labors desired or necessary on her part.

The same natural law extends to the intellectual province of woman. The average brain of woman, although of finer texture, is neither so heavy, nor are its tissues so strong, as that of man. There are some manifestations of mind in which she is superior to man. There is more delicacy of feeling, more modesty, more sensibility, more love, more vivacity. There have been in the same ages, few, if any equals in pathos, to Sappho and Mrs. Browning. But the epic, the comic, the practical, the profound, are seldom met with in the literary labors of women. As God has constituted the sexes, these are not to be expected. Where intense study, and long sustained effort, as upon the piano, which is woman's instrument, is required, man must achieve the accomplishment, and become the instructor. In sweetness of voice, and delicacy of modulation, the woman excels, but the bass voice, which is necessary in public speech, is not possible to the vocal organs of the woman. If God has indicated any thing in the construction of the vocal organs of the different sexes, it is easy for those who seek human good, to know the divine will, and it is unnatural and wicked to urge women to err on this subject.

Not only in general structure and in voice, but even in clothing, and in hair, nature, as well as revelation, has distinguished the male from the female. And this difference is observable in all species, from the insect to the mammal. In the human genus the hair of the male is coarse, and grows upon the face as upon the head. In all species below man, the clothing of the female is distinguishable in form, and often in color. There is sin against nature as well as revelation, on the part of those who urge men and women to transgress the laws of nature, and the principles of taste and beauty, in the matter of apparel, and wearing of long hair, which is the "ornament of women," but "a shame unto men."

The marital differences are another argument against the occupancy of the same positions. Man begets and woman bears. The declamation of erratic minds can not alter the natural constitution of things; yet this constitution makes the province of the two sexes separate, and yet dependent. Whether the creation of woman from the flesh and bone of man be allegory, fact, or fiction, it teaches a profound truth. Woman is the complement of man, and needs the protection of man, and the affection of man, even as his own flesh. Every true woman, if circumstances do not prevent, desires to be a wife and a mother; the natural consequences to the contrary, notwithstanding. There are monstrosities among women, but in the normal condition of humanity, "the desire of woman is unto her husband." No woman or man fulfills the natural destiny of the sexes in any other relation; and if social reformers would aim at promoting this end, they would bring a blessing to their kind. The social law of the Moravian church, which provides for companions for each member, is worthy of universal prevalence. He is the benefactor of women who aims to construct society in such way that each good woman will have a good husband.

When the home is constituted, that home is most happy, where there is most unity of affection and will, as well as unity of interest. Whatever tends to weaken this unity in the family, brings a curse to the household. The sexes were created one, of one; created one man, but male and female; one united head, as parents of one family. So far as unprincipled, or wrong-headed women and men urge schemes that tend to break the unity and peace of home, they do what tends to consign woman to harlotry, concubinage, or celibacy; there is no alternative.

What then are the relative duties, rights, and wrongs, connected with this marital constitution of the sexes?

About thirty years of a woman's life, all the days of her unabated strength, she is confined mostly at home, as a wife and a mother. Health, modesty, motherhood, require this. True women, that have true husbands, rejoice in it. During this time she must be provided for, and cared for tenderly by her husband, as she cares for her children. This natural constitution of things, precludes the possibility of women entering the professions and trades, and competing with men for wages or precedence. It exalts woman above man, in that it gives her the highest vocation on earth, the home teacher, but it absolutely excludes her from labors that require continued attention out of her own dwelling.

There are some professions, and some trades, that ought to be open to women; and unmarried women might fill them sometimes better than the men who now occupy them. But every employer knows, when such engagements are made, that his best help may accept a call to leave her place just at the time her services are becoming valuable to him. A man entering the marriage relation, would become more reliable, a woman less so. Hence, so long as the male body and brain are the strongest; and so long as men alone can be depended on for continuous labor, wages will differ. The principles of Christianity, however, would concede to self-dependent women the same wages; although, in some cases, the service might be of less value. Christianity, as before stated, is the complement of Providence, requiring the strong to support the weak, and those that have, to impart to those that need; but the intense application and consecutive labor that church, state, or public business requires, is not for woman.

At least three-fourths of the business of man's life requires out-door travel of single persons, at all times, and in all places, bad and good. In view of this fact, surely none but weak and unwise persons would think of women as justices, constables, politicians, and legislators. The vote, however, implies all these. And would not a certain class of women desire places for themselves? and women for constables, instead of men? and would not certain parties grant them their "rights," and gain their influence thereby?

It would be a sorrowful experiment, but in the end, perhaps, it would be a benefit, if in some state woman's suffrage should be granted. The Gordian knot of the Malthusian problem would be solved in half a century, by such an experiment, if it were to become general. Men marry to enjoy the social affections of home. When women become politicians and voters, with the attendant consequences, there will be few marriages; and among those without Christian principle, the "murder of the innocents" will be more common than at present. It is known, that women of the world, and others destitute of conscience, destroy multitudes of their own unborn offspring rather than be confined at home, or forego the pleasures of fashionable life. If this be true now, what would be true then? A reaction would come on, as in the clamor for natural rights in the free-love excitement. But such an experiment would cost too much; and the demoralization of the sexes would not be retrieved for a century.

While I believe that the arguments, in behalf of enlarging woman's sphere of action, are generally true, and indicative of a good heart in those who urge them, I think otherwise in regard to the arguments for woman's suffrage. So far as I have noticed them, there is fallacy or misapplication in them all.*

* Recently we have an utterance from the most entertaining platform-preacher in the world. He said, "Men pretended to be afraid that woman would unsex herself; but could a man by rocking the cradle for one of his children become a woman? It is the extreme of namby-pamby nonsense. She was wool-dyed in God's colors, and could never wash out."

This inimitable preacher ought never to meddle with logic nor with texts from the epistle to the Romans. It is woman's province to rock the cradle and provide food for the babe; and it is man's duty to supply the cradle and provide food for the mother. When the sexes depart, except as an episode in family life, from these relations, the distinctions and duties which nature ordains are violated. This figurative import the preacher knows is all any one means by men or women unsexing themselves. A good cause does not depend on brilliant tricks with an audience.

It is said that there are weak men, both in mind and body; and there are some women who can talk and work in public matters better than most men. This is an ingenious deception. There are some men that can attend young children and do culinary labor better than most women; but such exceptions only prove the general rule to which they are opposed. Things can be done that are unnatural both by men and women. Some roosters cackle, and some hens crow; but what do such exhibitions indicate?

It is said that women might vote without interrupting their home engagements, as many men do. But voting is only the executive part of the voter's interest. Shop-talk and discussion, caucauses, torchlight processions and other matters that need not be named, precede voting. It is necessary that there should be two parties in a country, and such necessity will exist until the world is ruled by truth and justice; but woman was not created for party strife, and it will be a wrong to render her connection with it necessary.

If one were to say a man who gets drunk and beats his wife is a brute, the reply of a genius of this sort would be, Oh! no; that is namby-pamby; God made him a man, he is dyed in the wool; he cannot unman himself, and become a brute.

But, it will be said, that at home with her husband, there would be no cross-questions or discussions. Granted, but in such case the vote would be simply doubled, with no difference in the result. Women's voting can make no difference in the result of an election, only so far as they differ from their husbands and relatives. The idea of advancing public interest in this way, can be predicated only on the hope of differences between men and women at home.

"But there are unmarried women who are independent, and some who have no home, no friends." Yes; but many of this class are ignorant, and others are abandoned and reckless women, and their vote would foster and honor vice, and give strength to the bad men who vote now in the same direction.

It is said that women have rights to protect as women, and men can not impartially maintain these as legislators, or, that they will not do it. This is folly. To protect the interests of women is as much the interest of the legislator as to protect the interests of men. Are not women's interests men's interests? Do not men care for their wives, mothers, daughters, sisters, as much as they do for their male constituents?

I have discharged, to the best of my ability, the duties of a law-maker, and I know that the rights of women are more sacred in the regard of legislators than the rights of men. Men suffer from inadequate wages, and from want of employment, as do women; and, while it is true that when men suffer, women suffer with them; yet there is not a legislature in the Union, that, in case of equal suffering, would not relieve the women before the men. Just as in a sinking ship, men will see all the women removed from the vessel before they disembark themselves.

"But have not women property to be taxed, and ought she not to vote for those who are to tax it? Ought there to be 'taxation without representation?'" This plea is an adroit deception. The taxation is on the property, irrespective of whether men or women own it. If there is any property peculiar to women as a sex, it will always be taxed lighter than any other on the tax list. Taxation without representation, means only that no species of property in a country shall be taxed by a power where the property taxed is not represented. A legislature could not enact laws for or against the property of women, without, by the same act, legislating for or against the same species of property in men.

Besides, the ballot, in a free country, is not predicated on property. If it were, men would vote as corporations and aristocracies do, in proportion to the amount of their estate. Such a qualification has been required in some instances by some of the states; but it is a wrong principle. The vote is predicated on the poll tax, the maintenance of agriculture, commerce, and manufactures, and the defense of the state when thus constituted.

It is urged, with great confidence, that vices would be reformed if the women had a vote, and that the moral party in politics would gain by the moral influence of the women. If I believed this, I should probably be a convert to morals as against nature; but natural law, not natural impulse, and moral duty are one. If women had a vote, political necessities, in order to success, would urge all women to vote, even when modesty and condition forbade the exposure. Ignorant and unprincipled women would undoubtedly all crowd the women's poll, and vote the saloon ticket, and if the thinking, respectable portion did not go also and vote, the others would largely increase Satan's majority. Children, even in arms, would not prevent enterprising females, of a certain class, from being at the polls; and then if more retiring women did not go out *nolens volens*, the anti-conscience party would be a large gainer by the women's vote.

"But would not sober women, who have drunken husbands, vote against the husband, in favor of a temperance law?" Seldom, if ever. A wise wife would not try to reform her husband by opposing him in politics. It would not be difficult for her to understand that it would only drive him farther from her, and oftener into the saloon. Her hope would be to reform him by complying with his wishes; and on promise of reform, she would vote with him, against a temperance law. Besides, in ninety-nine out of a hundred, such wives would be persuaded, before election day, that the temperance law was an interference with liberty, and an incentive to drunkenness. But suppose the women should pass a temperance law or any law against the vote of the men, who would enforce it?

Perhaps it will be said, that in country districts, where immoral women are not numerous, great advantages would be gained. But in such cases women would vote with their husbands. Many of them would not vote at all, so that the numbers of modest and respectable women that would stay at home, compared with an equal number of another class that would never stay at home, would cause a large loss to the best side in politics.*

When it is said that men, who create and de-

* Perhaps the sketch of a popular physician, dramatized, will give a more life-like idea of the future of this question. Suppose it is election morning: Mr. Tiltman suggests to his wife—

T. My dear, I hope you'll vote early to day.

Mrs. T. Why Mr. T! are you crazy! would you have a woman in my condition go to the polls?

T. Well, but, my dear, both Bridget and Dorothea will go, and vote for that scoundrel that keeps the den on the corner.

Mrs. T. Well; you know I ought not to go.

T. Can't you prevail on Bridget to stay at home?

Mrs. T. You know we agreed not to influence or interfere with her religion or politics.

T. We ought not to have done it; she's under the influence of the priests, who always vote wrong; and besides all the Taurite women will turn out, no matter what their condition.

Mrs. T. I'm really surprised at you, Tiltman. Is this your woman's rights! Have you lost all respect for your wife. I can't go in my own apparel. It would be torn and jammed to pieces.

T. Can't I get a conveyance and go along, and protect you?

Mrs. T. You know they don't let men into our poll; and the Mellesians are so horrid! You heard how Mrs. Forward got

fend the institutions of a country, ought to assume the duty of managing the machinery of the government, it is replied, evidently without seeing the *non sequiter* in the statement: "Did not the women, in the war for liberty, do their part as well as the men?" Yes, they did their part often better than the men. But their part was not the men's part. As nurses, as hospital dispensers, they were better than most of the men thus employed. But all the machinery and labor of the government and the war, laws, railroads, houses, medicines, conveyance, protection, were provided for them, as they should have been, by their male protectors. They were taken as women, and set down to their appropriate work; and they did it to the credit of their country and their sex. To plead such precedents to work a great wrong to women by urging them out of their natural position, is worse than weakness of mind.

pushed down and her face scratched. She struck one of them but she has been sick ever since. Besides the woman guardians (female police) are all on the other side. I wouldn't go for the world. Mrs. Meekheart never goes, and says she never will.

T. Her husband ought to see to that.

Mrs. T. Her husband isn't a fool. If he should urge out such a delicate wife, he would be a brute.

T. Confound it!—Where's Bridget?

Mrs. T. Gone to the Tenth Ward to work for her cousin Bob's election. She's got over young Sam Roberts.—[Exit Mr. T.

But would there not be a benefit to the state by doubling the number of voters? There might be benefit that I do not perceive; but any one can see that the evils would be many. There would be the expense of increasing the vote without changing the issue. In legislatures a certain number on each side often pair off and go home, or do not vote. If fifty leave that are equally divided, the vote of the fifty that remain will show the same result as the vote of the one hundred would have done. "But," says one, "some women would not vote with their husbands." A few might not, but the vote of the profligate women would far overbalance these.

Another result would be the introduction of some women, not the best, as it is with men, into public places, and the amalgamation of this class of women, with the same class of men, would not produce the best results. A legislature, or any assemblage, composed of women with no husbands, or of women whose husbands were at home with the children, and of men with wives at home, or no wives, would work strange results, and attract an audience into the lobbies, just as the public speeches of women attract an audience to see the speaker.

"But is not Victoria Queen of Great Britain?" Yes; and has about as much to do with devising, or arguing, or executing the laws of the realm, as the woman in the moon. "But there was Catherine of Russia." Yes; whose affections were conquered by her generals; and Mary of England, and Isabella of Spain, and many others, good and bad, who were ruled by the priests; all of them a tax on the public treasury, while they had no more to do with making the laws, or executing them, than the Queen of England has.

When women leave their homes and travel on electioneering campaigns; when they are separated in politics, and in law courts, from their husbands; when marriage becomes a partnership; when women are met as politicians and controversialists, as the nature of party action now requires men to meet, in the hall and in the street, the respect which modern civilization requires for woman will cease, and men will reply to their vituperations in terms that they use to each other, and which we will not now permit to be applied to our sisters, or our wives.

A vixen writer of marked ability, after telling gentlemen their duty, and prescribing their sphere, scolds like a Jezebel, because a writer, who is a husband and father, advises women to seek usefulness in home, rather than in public duties. She forgets that nature determines the question of home duties for women, and when they are advised by their friends to seek usefulness in the family, or in some light labor, it is merely advising them not to be unnatural in their hearts and habits. When a woman does unsex herself, no wise man will invite her to be mistress of a home; and a woman who has a home, will dishonor her husband, and neglect appropriate duties, if she assumes to discharge the services for which masculine functions are required. The man who advises a woman to attempt to sing bass, is an evil counsellor; either his motive or his mind is wrong.*

* I was present recently at a meeting of the queer company that assembled at the Cooper Institute, to advocate woman's rights. A note was read from the editor of the Independent, who is both a genius, and a radical reformer. The purport of the note was: "As I share my loaf with my wife, I am willing to share my vote with her." Neither Mr. Tilton, nor his feminine admirers, seemed to see the shallowness of what was designed to be smart sentiment. Mr. T. shares his vote with his wife now, as much as he does his loaf. When his wife votes, he will have a loaf, but no vote, to share with her. She will have her own vote then: ought she to have her own loaf too?

When the teaching of the New Testament on this subject is spoken of, it is a common remark of this newspaper writer to say

The writer referred to, thinks it a conclusive argument in behalf of women going to the polls that husbands and wives sometimes choose different religious denominations, while their different views and actions do not hinder their usefulness or happiness at home. The illustration is at fault; and if it were true, the conclusion drawn from it would be erroneous. It is not true that different denominational action is like different political action in the heads of a family. In different denominations each labors for the same Head of the church, and their hearts are united to the same leader. If they differed in politics, they would labor for opposing leaders,

that the import of the text is obsolete as the requirements to pray for Kings. Charity hopes that the writer does not perceive the perversion of Scripture in this oft repeated solecism. The word 'Kings' is used only as signifying office; and any other word designating official authority as president or governor, might be put in its stead; this the succeeding clause shows. But the instruction of the apostles in regard to woman's sphere and woman's duties are in the form of special precepts, the predicate of which cannot be varied in any respect. "Wives submit yourselves unto your own husbands, as unto the Lord. For the husband is the head of the wife, even as Christ is the head of the church." Now, whatever such passages may mean, we cannot put wife instead of husband, and affirm that the husband shall submit to the wife, and that the wife is the head of the husband. They mean, at least, what nature teaches, that God has constituted the husband the controling will in regard to general interests of the family.

and opposing interests. Besides, religious unity, which is strength, is not gained for either denomination; and the home division has almost invariably an injurious effect upon children.

There is a certain class of women now sometimes met with at the public boarding houses of the general and state governments, whose character is not like that of Mrs. Polk, and others who might be named; women whose influence radiated from their homes and was felt by the very best class of public men. Nor have the women spoken of the character of lady correspondents of newspapers, who often maintain a womanly deportment, while, they expose vice and commend virtue in high places. They are women with male idiosyncrasies; or they come as the stool-pigeons of men who have ends to gain. They send their notes; and novelty, as well as courtesy, and sometimes other motives, incline members to visit them, or to permit themselves to be visited. Under these circumstances the man hears and assents to their views or seems to do so. But this is neither well nor wise. Petitions from women, and their just claims, whether presented in person or otherwise, will always be heard. But a certain class of legislators deceive a certain class of women; and there will always be a few ultra radicals who will sympathize with wrong schemes, presented in the name of the right.

I have known women in the lobby, laboring for impracticable or unwise projects. Men would dine with them, talk with them, walk with them, assent to their projects; even bring in a bill professedly to accomplish their desire; but with the understanding among themselves that it was to be put adroitly out of the way. When women seek political ends, by personal suasion, with public men, there will generally be either sham, or fraud, or sin connected with such negotiations. There are thousands of easy minds in the world who sign petitions asking suffrage for women; and there are weak members in the legislature, for the first time, who are inclined to grant petitions, not remembering that nine tenths of the best women in the land condemn both the petition and the measure for which it asks.

We predict that no such event as women at the polls will ever take place over any considerable extent of the union. When it does occur, the ballot should be given first to the unmarried women. There is not one married woman in a hundred that would accept the ballot understanding the circumstances in which it would involve her. If it were forced upon women as a sex, in ten years there would be a universal presentation of petitions from christian families, to be relieved from the useless and injurious operation of a state of things which gave profligacy and badly organized minds the ascendancy, and militated against the privacy of the family, the duties of a wife, and the modesties of motherhood.

CHAPTER XVI.

CAPITAL PUNISHMENT

There is a class of reformers who are moved by their sympathies, rather than by the reason and justice of the case. This class of men sometimes become dangerous to the well-being of society. They sympathize with scoundrels, and seek to save them from just penalties. They would make the penitentiary a place of comfortable retirement for villains, and thus induce such a state of things, that those who had never been there, would have no dread of the crime that would send them there; and those who had been there would be prepared for any villainy, if going back to light labor and comfortable quarters was the only consequence. To provide for the health and moral reform of criminals, is proper, but to make their penalty a punishment is a duty, which it is crime against society to neglect. We have had some experience in framing legislative provisions and penalties for criminals, and I am sure that the policy that makes a penitentiary more comfortable in labor and quarters than an honest day laborer can afford, is a premium offered for crime.

The persons alluded to may be called instinctive reformers, because their impulses are organic, not moral. They frequently misdirect their compassion, because the impulse, in their case, is the highest law. They oppose capital punishment, and denounce those who maintain the justice of the death penalty. They do this in common *ad captandum* phrase, appealing to the sense of sympathy, not to the sense of justice. Now, while it is admitted that none but the willful and deliberate murderer should die, it has not been shown that the Scriptures, or the principles of mercy guided by justice and reason, would permit the deliberate murderer to live. He has shown himself to be the enemy of his race, and should be separated from them either by painless death, or by life imprisonment without hope of pardon.

There is a vicious sympathy that excuses itself towards the guilty rather than the innocent. A sympathy opposed to the just suffering of criminals is suspicious. Suppose I witness a pirate-ship attack a packet, and murder in cold blood the crew and passengers. Immediately after, a revenue-cutter attacks the pirate, and destroys the murderers of the innocent. There was as much of animal suffering in the one case as the other. But if I feel for the sufferings of the pirates as I do for the murdered passengers, I am a brute, possessing blind compassion without a sense of justice; or else I am a pirate at heart, sympathizing with like character.

It is painful to read the remarks of such sympathizers, when they talk mawkishly about the momentary suffering of the murderer, while not a word is said, and apparently not an emotion felt, in view of the various, protracted, and excruciating sufferings which the villain may have inflicted upon his innocent victim.

It is an error to place the mercy of the New Testament in antagonism to capital punishment. The Scriptures recognize an abatement in severity and frequency of penalty, as light, and civil security increases in the world. Efforts to prevent crime and reform the criminal will increase with the advances of christianity; but the cardinal principles of the Christian Scriptures recognize the rectitude of the voluntary suffering of individuals, when it is necessary for the good of the whole, and of penal infliction when necessary as penalty for violated law. Even the death-penalty is recognized as proper when executed as a penalty for crime worthy of death. Paul says, "If I have done any thing worthy of death, I refuse not to die." Thus implying that such crimes were possible, and such penalty proper. The Mosaic institutions were for a peculiar people, in the initiatory stages of civilization and piety; but the Great Teacher sanctioned the death penalty under the law of Moses, and thereby taught that taking life as a penalty is not wrong in itself. Hence the true inference is, that while it may be proper under the gospel to abate the death-penalty in all minor cases of crime and perhaps in the end substitute therefor life-labor without hope of reprieve, yet the infliction of the death-penalty on the part of society can never be shown to be wrong in itself. Jesus said to the Scribes and Pharisees who had abrogated the death-penalty in the case of the drunken, stubborn, and rebellious son that cursed his parents, and could not be reformed, Matt. 15, "God commanded, saying, Honor thy father and thy mother, and he that curseth father or mother let him die the death; but ye say otherwise, and thus make the commandment of God of none effect."

The ultimate principle, admitted by all, is, that as life is the highest individual good, it should be protected by the highest penalty. If no other than the death-penalty will so certainly protect the life of the innocent, then those who would spare the life of the murderer, do it at the expense of the life of the innocent. Now it has never been proved, and can not be, that in the present state of society imprisonment for life is a security against future murder by the condemned. A criminal was condemned by a jury to be hung for deliberate murder, in the state of Ohio, a few years since. This penalty was commuted to imprisonment for life. In less than three years, afterwards he was pardoned; and for the crimes he has since committed, the sympathizers with this murderer are guilty.

Commutation, or sentence to life imprisonment, endangers witnesses both before and after trial. A man of fifty commits a theft. He knows an imprisonment of ten years will follow the proof. Will he not thus be bribed to murder the witness? His penalty for both crimes can be no greater than that for the least; and if he murders the witness he hopes to escape. Will not the discontinuance of the death penalty transform most thieves into murderers? That it has done so in many cases, is in evidence in confessions and in criminal courts. If men commit the murder it is only imprisonment for a longer term, and that penalty doubtful; if they kill their victim, his testimony is impossible, and chances of escape are greater, while the penalty is in many cases no greater. Will it not take away from the public mind an impression of the sanctity of life, and thus in the estimation of villains decrease their sense of the guilt of murder? A virtuous community will punish the guilty. An immoral community will punish them by impulse, or not at all. The remission of the death-penalty has produced in Wisconsin, and is now producing in some other States, many unlawful outrages. The conscience which God has given men says, the murderer should die. This has been its testimony in all ages and in all time. When an immoral philanthropy remits the death-penalty, natural conscience is outraged, and men rise in mobs to inflict vengeance upon the murderer.

The pleas usually urged against the death-penalty have slight foundation either in morals or in reason. It is said that in some cases the innocent suffer death, and no remuneration can be made. So they may suffer imprisonment for life, and no remuneration can be made. Imperfection may attach to all law and penalty that is based upon testimony; but even this possible evil might be guarded against by sentence of imprisonment, without pardon, when doubt of the fact were possible.

It is said, again, that society, when it takes life for life, commits the same crime with the malefactor. Shame on such solecisms; then when we confine a murderer for life, we commit a crime equal in guilt to that of the criminal. When society takes a certain sum as penalty from a man who damaged his neighbor, it commits the same offense with the criminal; if there were a society of criminals for the promotion of crime, such arguments would receive a premium.

But it is sometimes said that life is sacred;

it ought not to be taken in any case; it can be forfeited only to Him who gave it. The statement is false in fact and in theory. If any man were attacked by an assassin, with deadly weapons, and with the known intent to kill, it would be his duty to save his own life by taking the life of the murderer. Now, is not life forfeited as much after the act as before? It is certain that the guilt is as great, and that justice and universal conscience would affirm the same penalty after, as before the fact. If the murderer escapes, is society guilty for doing what the murdered man ought to have done?

It is said society is guilty in view of the imperfect provision made for the moral and intellectual training of the masses of the people. If our school systems be inadequate or partial, they should be reformed and strengthened; but this, while it would prevent the development of evil, in many cases, would not prevent crime. It is a fallacy to argue that the absence of remedies used to prevent an evil is the cause of that evil. If the argument were true, all who have inadequate intellectual and moral training would be alike criminals; which statement is false and slanderous.

It is said, again, by the philosophers of the Fowler school, that the propensity to crime is organic; that criminal acts arise from the unbalanced impulsion of certain cranial developments; and that therefore the criminal should be an object of pity rather than a subject for penalty, because his impulse is natural. If this be true, then the Calvinistic system, which these reformers take pains to deride, is true in its utmost stringency. If this were true, then murderers should be exterminated for the same reason that we kill a viper or a tiger. Both are the natural enemies of human life; and reform in any case would be just as possible as in the other. The Chinese, who kill both the criminal and his children to prevent the natural propagation of crime, would be right. Such a philosophy ignores reform efforts of all kinds. Reform in that case would be possible only by knocking in the evil developments on the head. The Fowler philosophy perpetrates the error of all superficial thinking. It takes facts, true only as a general expression, and derives particulars from them. It likewise applies its principles wrong-end foremost. It makes development govern mind instead of urging the true application, that it is the character of the mind that produces the peculiarities of development in the body. The seed produces the tree, not the tree the seed. A bad spirit produces bad developments. The law of creation and of philosophy agrees with the Scriptures that "every seed produces its own body, and 'so it will be in the resurrection.'"

But it is argued that murderers dread imprisonment for life as much as they do the gallows. All facts, and all consciousness in all men, deny this assertion. If this be true, why do criminals and their friends seek a commuting of penalty? Why do all murderers joyfully accept commutation? Even the devil concedes the falsehood of this statement when he said, "All that a man hath will he give for his life."

Penalty is designed to prevent as well as to punish crime. The death-penalty is the highest restraint that can possibly be opposed to murder. Murder is unlike all other crimes. It is the crime of crimes: but it can never be distinguished as such without inflicting upon the murderer the highest penalty. By the death-penalty the murderer is taught to value the life of others as he does his own. This is the golden rule. And unless death be the penalty, a villain meditating crime can never value the life of another as he does his own. By the imprisonment-penalty he is taught to value the life of his neighbor as little as he values imprisonment in the penitentiary. Who dares to teach murderers this low estimate of life?

It is said that facts and statistics prove that imprisonment is a remedy as effectual in preventing murder as the death-penalty. This is not proved; and I believe it is not true. Facts, as far as they go, prove the contrary. The instances alleged in favor of abolishing the death-penalty, those of Catharine of Russia and the government of Tuscany, were of too short duration to prove any thing. On the other side, we have the case in the German States, where the statistics are accurate, and sufficient time for a fair experiment has been allowed. The "Conversation-Lexicon," a work of the highest authority concerning German topics, says, "Those States where, from a one-sided benevolence, the government wished to abolish capital punishment, were compelled again to avail themselves of it, and that on the ground that in the opinion of men death is the greatest of evils, in preference to which they would willingly undergo the most laborious life, with some hopes of escape from it, because the death-penalty is the most terrible of penalties."

Wordsworth, a man of the most highly-endowed intellect, the purest and the warmest benevolence, in the London Quarterly Review, says: "Whenever it appears to be good for mankind, according to the arrangements of Providence, that death should be inflicted by human ministration, it is a false humility, a false humanity, and false piety, for a man to refuse to be the instrument."*

Robespierre resigned his office in early life rather than sign a warrant for the execution of a criminal. He exhibited a nature sympathetic to criminals, but his future life showed him to be a monster, destitute by nature of the sense of justice.

The following passage in Blackstone, Book IV. chap. 1., should not be forgotten: "In France the punishment of robbery, either with or without murder, is the same; hence it is that though perhaps they are subject to fewer robberies, yet they never rob but they also murder.

* See Cheever on Capital Punishment.

In China murderers are cut to pieces, but robbers not; hence in that country they never murder on the highway, though they often rob." Is not this satisfactory proof that the man, or the legislature, that, through sympathy with criminals, aids to abolish the death-penalty, thereby stimulates villains to murder the innocent.

If this is not sufficient, take a fact nearer home. Capital punishment was abolished several years since in Michigan. The grand jury of Wayne County in that State made a presentment to the legislature, in which they say: "Facts, we are informed, have occurred in our midst, proving that some of the murderers in this county have been influenced and urged forward to their deeds of wickedness, through the consideration that the death-penalty has been abolished from our penal code."

Much might be added, showing that in the present state of society, imprisonment for life is often a bribe to commit murder; in other cases it is no penalty; and in all cases it places the murderer where no further penalty for crime is possible. He may murder his keeper; he may poison the prison well, and thus murder all the inmates; his life is sacred, and he is above law; no further penalty can be inflicted.

The Bible nowhere teaches that willful murderers ever exercise repentance unto life. "No murderer hath eternal life abiding in him." That murderers repent, no one doubts. Judas repented and went to "his own place." Repentance is either selfish or holy. If it is repentance in view of the consequence to one's self, it produces remorse, or deceives the mind. Every criminal repents when the hand of the sheriff is on his shoulder. This is forced repentance. It is the murderer's repentance. It is not honest repentance. But it is "repentance unto death." Not holy repentance, produced by faith in Christ.

Some, I know, believe that true repentance in such cases is possible. If it be possible, the death-penalty is much more likely to produce repentance than the penalty of imprisonment. Dr. Webster, the Boston murderer, while there was hope of escape or commutation, maintained the falsehood that he was innocent. When sentence was passed, and pardon or commutation denied, he became penitent and truthful. In "Bemis' Report," of Webster's last conversation with the sheriff he says: "All the proceedings in my case have been just. The court have discharged their duty. The law officers of the commonwealth did their duty, and no more. The verdict of the jury was just. The sentence of the court was just; and it is just that I should die on the scaffold, in accordance with that sentence." Thus does the sentence of death when there is no hope of escape, produce in some cases, honest repentance. As in Webster's statement that his sentence was just, and that he deserved to die, we have the same evidence given in many other cases when the crime is confessed. It is the decision of the human conscience, one which ought not to be violated, that the man who deliberately takes the life of his neighbor forfeits his own. The man who from sympathy with criminals, refuses to award this highest penalty to the highest crime, manifests a corrupted sympathy, rejects the decisions of the conscience, and the conviction of human reason in all past ages, and in some cases strengthens the hands of the guilty against the innocent.

We have now traveled over the Philosophical, the Theological, and Reform view of the times, and have occasionally referred to those who are affiliated with the abnormal moral movements to which we allude. We have endeavored to separate the pure from the vile, and to reject nothing good, while we repudiated the evil. Perhaps we have, in our desire to grant all that charity demanded, allowed some things to stand as truth, which the better-informed may condemn as error. We have done what we could. To God and sincere inquirers we commend the effort.

Bible Lands. With Glimpses of

EUROPE AND EGYPT. By S. Dryden Phelps, D.D., Author of "Sunlight and Heart-light," Poems for the "Heart and Home," etc. 12mo. 450 pages. Retail price. $2.00.

It is beautifully illustrated with more than twenty pictures, all telling some significant truth, or illustrating some important fact. The reader, taking this volume in hand, passes in clear and rapid march throughout Europe, seeing the most important objects and personages of the present and past, until he feels really as though he had been there in person. So with Egypt, that wonderful land; so with all the Bible Lands most wonderful in history. No Bible student, especially no Sabbath-school teacher, can afford to be with out this book. Dr. Phelps writes in a condensed, yet in a beautiful style, which you read without weariness. This work covers as much ground as some others which are much larger and more expensive.

"A new book of travels, and a good one; a luxury to enjoy."—*The Observer, N. Y.*

"In a full, rich volume, with twenty admirable illustrations, the author and publishers have well performed their parts. The eye of a poet, the mind of a well-read scholar, and the warm, enthusiastic heart of a Christian pastor, have combined to give this rich treat. Some of our ministers are warmly commending this book to their flocks."—*Watchman and Reflector, Boston.*

"Dr. Phelps blends, in his account of the scenes and localities of Scripture, the most child-like simplicity of faith with poetic fervor and manly intelligence. The joyous faith of the book is beautiful."—*The Methodist.*

"Short, terse, correct, and clear, it commends itself to home and Sunday-school readers."—*N. W. Christian Advocate, Chicago.*

"He gives us an agreeable book—is a thoughtful observer and a pleasant writer; his experiences are fresh and his observations recent. His book has nothing sectarian in its views."—*Springfield Republican.*

"With this volume in hand, with its vivid descriptions, rich illustrations, its skillful selection of those themes most fertile in intellectual, poetic, and spiritual interest, one can sit by his fireside and enjoy not a little of the romance of travel, while his mind is enriched by the reflections of an accomplished scholar, whose imagination has been trained to the appreciation of all that is sublime and beautiful." John S. C. Abbott.

For sale by all Booksellers, or sent by mail for retail price, by

CLARKE & CO.,
Publishers, Chicago, Ill.

"Splendid New Books for Boys and Girls."

CECIL'S BOOKS OF NATURAL HISTORY

IN THREE VOLUMES. CECIL'S BOOK OF BEASTS; CECIL'S BOOK OF BIRDS; CECIL'S BOOK OF INSECTS. 16mo, 200 pages each. Handsomely illustrated with 33 full page engravings. Retail price, $1.25 per volume; in sets, $3.50.

The writer has not prepared a compendium of Natural History, but has endeavored to present, in a clear and familiar style, neither puerile nor abstruse, pleasing descriptions of several of the most interesting families in each department of animated nature. Whether talking about owl or squirrel, bat, beaver, bee, or beetle, facts have been verified by observation or upon reliable authority, incidents are real, inferences natural and legitimate. Each book is complete in itself, and in harmony with the rest of the series; contains about 200 pages, 16mo. beautifully printed on fine book paper, and is profusely illustrated with engravings on wood, prepared in the highest style of the art, especially for this work. These books are among the best of THE JUVENILES, either for gifts, for general reading, or for Sabbath-school libraries.

"Cecil's Books of Natural History, three illustrated volumes by Selim H. Peabody, A. M., are both interesting and instructive and are widely read East and West, and are most excellent books to put into the hands of the young."—*Watchman and Reflector, Boston, Mass.*

"He writes with great good taste, uses admirable discretion in the selection of facts, and makes, in every chapter, a story which we are sure both old and young will find attractive. In the great dearth of really good books for children, we commend this series as one of the best, a model in its way."—*The Daily Tribune, Chicago.*

"Each of these books is complete in itself, and all are chapters in the great book of natural history. They are written in fine taste and are well adapted to the juvenile mind."—*North American, Phil. Pa.*

"They should be in every Sabbath School Library, and read by every boy and girl in the country. If parents and teachers would take more pains to put such books into the hands of children they would not so often have their tastes perverted by reading "Ten Cent Novels." We heartily commend the Books."—*Indiana Teacher, Indianapolis, Ind.*

For sale by all Booksellers, or sent by mail for retail price, by

CLARKE & CO.,

Publishers, Chicago, Ill.

www.ingramcontent.com/pod-product-compliance
Lightning Source LLC
LaVergne TN
LVHW010211110826
845151LV00004B/1058
* 9 7 8 1 4 2 5 5 2 8 4 6 1 *